Praise for
Tasting Grace

"Using stories of her own triumphs and pain, Melissa digs past the surface layers of food as we see it on television, in cookbooks, and on social media. She helps us think about it in a whole new way—as nothing short of a spiritual force, a vessel through which we can experience (and extend) compassion, comfort, fellowship, love, enjoyment, and grace."

—REE DRUMMOND, author of *The Pioneer Woman Cooks*

"The intersection between faith and food is endlessly interesting to me, and Melissa articulates the significance and beauty of that intersection so well. She is a great storyteller, and she invites us into her story and gives us a seat at her table with graciousness and wisdom."

—SHAUNA NIEQUIST, *New York Times* best-selling author of
Present Over Perfect and *Bread and Wine*

"These aren't just words on pages; they are an invitation to a feast, to hospitality, and to finding lasting purpose in your life. Melissa has set a table fit for a King, pulled our chairs, and reminded us there's a place for us here. This is a book that will feed not only your imagination but also your soul."

—BOB GOFF, author of *New York Times* bestseller *Love Does*

"I have loved Melissa for years, and *Tasting Grace* reminds me why. She combined virtually all my favorite things—food, family, fabulous stories, God—and made me want to race into my kitchen and accept her beautiful invitations to nourish my mind and soul and family by cooking."

—JEN HATMAKER, *New York Times* best-selling author of *For
the Love*

"In *Tasting Grace,* d'Arabian invites us to take a personal journey into the deep meaning of eating and to discover the power of food to illuminate and heal life. This book will help you taste food and savor life in ways you may not have thought possible."

—NORMAN WIRZBA, author of *Food and Faith*

"In *Tasting Grace,* Melissa traces the movements of God in her life through food. It's a gift to be offered a peek 'behind the scenes'—to witness God's presence in both the tender moments and the glamorous ones."

—KENDALL VANDERSLICE, author of *We Will Feast*

"Ever since I won *The Next Food Network Star,* Melissa has been my source of big-sister wisdom on everything from career roller coasters to motherhood surprises to Bible study. Believe me, the Melissa I know is the exact same Melissa you'll find in this book. Just a few chapters in, she had already unraveled my own latent, long-held belief that my relationship with food is some kind of wild stallion to be tamed rather than an invitation from God to understand how he loves his children. By the end, I found myself looking at food with new eyes—as sustenance not just for my body but also for my soul."

—AARTI SEQUEIRA, chef, television personality, journalist, and author

"In a voice unparalleled in its warmth, humor, and wisdom, Melissa shares personal stories and insights that inspire the reader not only to create delicious food and the meaningful connections that shared meals generate but also to be attentive to what fresh pastures their own God-given longings may be calling them toward. Highly and warmly recommended."

—RACHEL MARIE STONE, author of *Eat with Joy*

"Melissa invites everyone to the table in this creative and rich book. Fans will love the behind-the-scenes peek into her life experiences with food, and everyone will benefit from her inspiring take on what food is meant to be."

—RICHARD BLAIS, chef, entrepreneur, and television personality

MELISSA D'ARABIAN

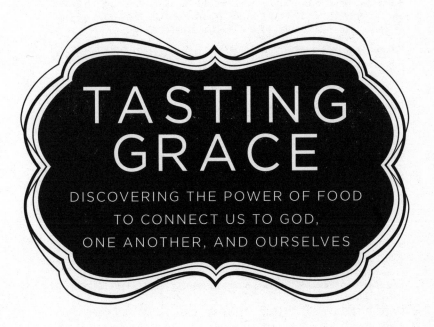

TASTING GRACE

DISCOVERING THE POWER OF FOOD
TO CONNECT US TO GOD,
ONE ANOTHER, AND OURSELVES

WATERBROOK

Hardcover ISBN 978-0-525-65273-1
eBook ISBN 978-0-525-65274-8

Copyright © 2019 by Melissa d'Arabian

Cover design by Kelly L. Howard

Library of Congress Cataloging-in-Publication Data
Names: D'Arabian, Melissa, author.
Title: Tasting grace : discovering the power of food to connect us to God, one another, and ourselves / Melissa d'Arabian.
Description: First Edition. | Colorado Springs : WaterBrook, 2019. | Includes bibliographical references.
Identifiers: LCCN 2018059414 | ISBN 9780525652731 (hardcover) | ISBN 9780525652748 (electronic)
Subjects: LCSH: Christian women—Religious life. | Food—Religious aspects—Christianity.
Classification: LCC BV4527 .D345 2019 | DDC 248.8/43—dc23
LC record available at https://lccn.loc.gov/2018059414

Printed in the United States of America
2019—First Edition

10 9 8 7 6 5 4 3 2 1

For Philippe, Océane, Margaux,
Charlotte, and Valentine.
You make it all matter.

Contents

How Is God Reaching Us Through Food?

Food, as well as our relationship to food, is central to modern-day life. As a society, we are infatuated with recipes and food photos; chefs are celebrities; today's TV programming is filled with shows about food: competitions, guides, and exposés—and not just on niche websites or cable networks, but everywhere we look, including prime-time mainstream network television. Bookstores are filled not only with cookbooks, which have become more visual escapes than actual instruction manuals, but with entire tomes about food, life in food media, behind-the-scenes glimpses into food careers, and culinary travel guides. When we aren't talking about food directly—debating veganism, the value of organic food, how much or little it should be cooked, and where it can be sourced—we focus on the management of food in our lives: how to lose weight as well as how often, how much, and what kinds of food to eat or avoid and in what combinations for optimum health. Health and weight issues aside, we're so obsessed with food that it is styled up and made impossibly pretty for the masses, creating a culture of food elitism or, more crassly, food porn. Food is at the very core of our daily lives.

Food isn't just a big part of modern society; it's central throughout history, particularly in many key biblical moments. From the beginning, which we see in Genesis, God designed a food system—his process for feeding us—as part of creation. Food was central to man's first obedience and man's first disobedience (anyone else shout "Don't touch that apple, Adam!" when you read Genesis?). In Exodus, God delivered bread, or manna, to the Israelites. Isaiah is where we first read about the promise that, at the end of time, the Lord will host his people at a lavish banquet (the "messianic banquet"). And food is all over the New Testament! Jesus ate and drank throughout his ministry (noted more in Luke than in any of the other gospels), and he used meals to feed the hungry, welcome the marginalized, and offer his body as the Bread of Life. Meals were a cornerstone of the early church. In fact, they *were* the early church services. Believers worshipped and broke bread together daily. These are just a few examples that make one thing clear: *food was not an afterthought for God.*

God's Invitations for Us

As Christians, we commonly think of meals in terms of their ability to bring together a community, and that is right and good. But looking at food through the lens of the Bible tells us a meal does so much more. Food invites us into God's creation, is a cornerstone of hospitality, guides us into compassion, reminds us to slow down, is a source of delight and connection, is an opportunity to lean into our dependence on God, and motivates us to accept ourselves and the oneness of humankind or creature-kind. Food fuels far more than our bodies; it drives ministry, marks celebrations, and connects us to our true selves, to one another, and to God himself.

Turns out, God has a lot to say through food, and it's not all in line with what society is saying about food. Before I wrote this book—in fact, what led me to writing it!—I prayed, read, cooked, studied Scripture, and listened. And I remembered experiences from across my life that shaped who I am as a food professional, a mom, a wife, and a woman. I came to respect the role food has in our lives in general and in mine in particular, a role far bigger than I had expected. When I took the time to consider the powerful place food has had in my life, I saw how intertwined food and God were, and patterns—*lessons* I even called them—emerged.

I have a somewhat complicated history with food. Most people know me from Food Network's reality show *The Next Food Network Star* (which I won in its fifth season) or from my subsequent cooking show *Ten Dollar Dinners*. But what most people don't know is that I grew up not always having enough, which shaped my views on food when I was a child. Then, as a woman, I took in the many mixed messages of this world and found myself stuck in a no-man's-land of wanting to eat healthy but somehow slipping into eating to get thinner rather than to make my body its best temple for God. There is a fine line between eating healthy and exercising in worship of God and eating healthy and exercising because I want to be pretty or admired by the world. The two approaches look very similar. But they are different in a crucial way: one is worshipping the Creator, and the other is worshipping the world he created. And that is the tension we are living with: what society says about food isn't necessarily what God says about food, and if we aren't paying attention, we can fall into the world's ways.

As I progressed in my quest to understand how God is using food in my life, hoping that some of my experience would speak to you too, I softened. God's meals weren't lessons of admonition; they were welcoming me to be closer to him. They were invitations simply waiting to be opened.

God used food to invite me into his love.

This book is the story of those invitations.

And God is inviting you into the same love—and using food as a way to connect with you.

Consider Me a Trench Buddy

We're all busy. I get it. I'm a working mom who always has more items on my to-do list than hours in the day. I've been there when the schedule is so packed that the easiest thing is to grab a quick meal or snack and head off to the next thing without ever giving my food choice or God's invitation a thought. Been there?

That's why I wrote this book: to help us all hear God's invitation a little more clearly, to sift through the food-frenzied culture, and to listen to how God yearns for us to use and appreciate what he has created for us. At the end of each chapter, in a section called "RSVP to the Invitation," I've shared some of the activities that helped me find my way to God's invitations. I hope you find them as helpful as I did.

Some people know me as a Food Network "star" or from my weekly Associated Press "Healthy Plate" column. However, I'm not in the food business or even in the TV business. I'm in the business of being in the trenches with other women, sharing our experiences to make our lives a little bit easier and a lot more meaningful. I'm a trench buddy, because we all want someone to understand what it means to try to feed her family and create a life of significance, someone who won't pile on a heap of guilt for not creating gourmet meals and designing amazing, magazine-cover-worthy food presentations. Over the ten years I have been on television, I have become known for my family and faith just as much as for my recipes and kitchen tips. You and I are in this together—on a quest not just for healthy and inexpensive ways to feed ourselves and our families, but also to navigate the hype and find God's truth for us in every meal, snack, drink, and grocery aisle.

My first two books—*Ten Dollar Dinners* and *Supermarket Healthy*—were, on the surface, a budget cookbook and a healthy cookbook. But to me they were both spiritual books, rooted in gratitude and stewardship. *Ten Dollar Dinners* isn't about getting the cheapest thing you can find in the store, but it celebrates God's seasonality and shares smart strategies for getting the most for our hard-earned money. *Supermarket Healthy* isn't a diet book; it reminds us that food nourishes our families, so let's feed them mindfully. I wrote them with my Bible open, and I found inspiration and direction in God's Word. Both of these books share my Christian worldview with a secular world.

I felt a strong calling to write my first Christian book a few years ago. I'd been leading Bible studies and speaking to and teaching Christian audiences for several years. But before I wrote an actual book, I longed for more formal study with professors and thought leaders. I felt that my reach with television was broader than my theological base and that my branches were wider than my roots were long. I began to study the Bible more deeply, in earnest, beyond my daily morning devotionals. In 2015, I completed a one-year certificate program in theology and ministry through Princeton Theological Seminary. If there is anything I learned from that year of deep study, it's how much more I have to learn! I continue to be a daily student of God's Word, wrestling with and digesting it to keep my life meaningful, significant, and on God's path for me. I also learned that I am an academic by nature, so I could easily keep studying as a stalling tactic instead of writing the book

God had placed in my heart! Which brings us to the book you're now holding. *Tasting Grace* will not be perfect, and if there are errors in the interpretation of God's Word on food, then those are mine alone. But this book has been dancing in my head in various forms for several years, and I'm relieved to have finally written it. I've lived every letter and every space in it. And now I offer it to you.

If you are reading this, you may be a lot like me—a Christian woman grappling with one of life's many thought-provoking seasons: new job or school, midlife, postbaby, empty nest, kids getting married. But I also hope if you aren't, you feel welcome anyway. Wherever we are in life, whatever our faith may be, I know we are connected simply by the fact that we share the same world and we all eat. We all know the edgy feeling of hunger pangs, some more acutely than others, and we all know the nourishing feeling of being well fed by food and by company.

I also imagine that you might see a bit of yourself in my struggles and questions. Struggles such as figuring out what kind of food is honoring your body—and where Diet Coke fits into the puzzle. Questions such as wondering how to feed your family while managing a budget. My hope is that we can connect over what we have in common, overcome and celebrate what we don't, and honor one another on our various paths. My hope is that we can start a deeper conversation about food and its power to bring us together, draw out the best in us, and hear God's voice in the midst of it all.

All of us crave trench buddies so we can share our deepest fears and hopes about ourselves and our families. Feeling inadequate and unworthy when it comes to our individual food stories is at the top of that list for many people, women perhaps even more than men. While *Tasting Grace* offers a lot of personal stories and honesty about my struggles with food, it is more than a food memoir. It's a hand reaching out from the trenches, opening the conversation that I think we should be having, and sharing the journey to consider these core questions:

How does my eating please God? Am I willing to trust his food vision for me?

I want to let go of what the world is saying about food and lean into God's creation. I invite you to join me.

Chapter 1

Hungering for What Truly Satisfies

An Invitation into Compassion

Jesus used food to bring people together
and to feed both bodies and souls.

ood saved me. This is a bold statement for a Christian girl like me.
But when you're hungry, in the literal empty-tummy sort of way,
spiritual hunger takes a back seat. Who would guess that God would
fill the second by filling the first? Yet isn't that what Jesus did? He used
food to connect with people and feed them the real nourishment: his
message of redemption.

When I was little, we lived on the east side of Tucson, Arizona, in
a rundown, two-bedroom adobe house with worn, stained carpet and
faded, sticky linoleum floors. Mom was raising my older sister, Stacy,
and me on a shoestring. She'd divorced my dad when I was just a few
months old. (Turns out, those quickie Vegas weddings when you're still
a teenager don't always end in happily ever after.) She was also putting

herself through college, living off student loans and a small teacher's assistant salary, and dreaming of attending medical school.

Like most kids, I figured our life was like everyone's. Despite its imperfections, our tiny house on East Silver Street was home. It was where we pulled up to the table for meals. It was where we knew we belonged.

When Stacy and I begged Mom for our own bedrooms, she let me move into the only space available: the utility room. We squeezed a twin mattress onto the floor of the narrow room. There was no space for a bed frame. The mattress fit only when the door was wedged half-open, pressing deep into the corner of my mattress. So that's how that bedroom stayed for years—with a door permanently stuck forty-five degrees open. Since my makeshift bedroom was the only way out to the backyard, anyone wanting to go outside had to shimmy around the wedged door, stepping on my mattress in the process. Our large dog, Joya, went back and forth at will through the humongous doggy door, and to this day I remember the *flip-flop* of that rubber flap going all night long.

Why we had a large, hungry dog when we could barely afford to feed the humans in the house remains a mystery. Somehow our mom couldn't say no to our animal-loving requests. We had pets aplenty: rabbits, parakeets, guinea pigs, cats, and—at a high (low?) point— thirty-eight chickens in our urban-zoned backyard. Mom sold the eggs, a carton at a time, to her classmates and professors to earn a few extra bucks a month.

Our mom loved Stacy and me deeply. We knew this in our bones. I remember the way she would stay up all night with me when I had chronic ear infections even though she had school the next morning. To this day, Mom was always my biggest fan. She constantly told me that my future was bright and that I could grow up to be anything I wanted. But she was stressed. Stressed about school . . . money . . . feeding us . . . raising us, all the while probably feeling—like most college students—barely an adult herself.

We ate simply, since Mom's cooking skills matched our sparse budget. Dinners were an unimaginative rotation of meat loaf, tacos, baked fish, and a weird black-eyed-pea-and-rice casserole that my mom inexplicably felt sophisticated serving. Her worn copy of *365 Ways to Cook Hamburger* was the only cookbook in our kitchen, unless you count *Diet for a Small Planet,* which was more of a trendy, hippy political statement for Mom than an actual source of recipes, the aforementioned black-eyed-pea dish being the exception.

Packing lunches was extra taxing. Finding portable options to send with us to school was just too much for Mom to deal with. So, as elementary school students, Stacy and I took over the task. We were ill equipped to turn the ingredients in our home—like a pound of frozen hamburger meat—into brown-bag meals. We could afford only the very cheapest lunch meat—a slim, plastic envelope of processed meat pressed so thin that our one-see-through-slice-per-sandwich portion couldn't have added a full gram of protein to any sandwich unlucky enough to receive it. And when the weekly lunch meat ration ran out, we turned to an apple or an orange or some aging, floppy celery for lunch. My sister and I were allocated one napkin a day to share at dinnertime, so the apple-for-lunch day usually left me with sticky fingers and chin that remained throughout recess. Sometimes we'd wrap up dry cornflakes in awkward wax paper—Saran Wrap was too pricey for everyday use—and have that for our meal.

My school's lunchroom was where I first realized we were poor. What we eat speaks volumes about where we sit in the societal pecking order, created largely by accidents of birth and geography, and the cafeteria made me aware of that hierarchy. Other kids' lunches smelled like peanut butter sandwiches mingled with overripe bananas. My classmates brought prepackaged goodies every day, oblivious to the miracle in which they were participating. I remember vividly a classmate named Katy Rudder because she shared her daily bag of deliciously salty Fritos with me, unaware that I counted on her corn chips to help fill my empty belly. More than just sharing her meal, Katy shared the table with me, saving me a spot I called my own, no matter what flimsy lunch I toted—or didn't—to school.

From that spot in the cafeteria, I quietly marveled at the students who brought multiple courses in brown bags not only labeled with their names but decorated, too, with cute hearts or loopy smiley faces drawn by their moms. They might even find a sticker or a little note to go with their carefully prepared meal. Baggies, Saran Wrap, and foil all spoke the language of the lunch-packing elite of my lower-middle-class neighborhood. I quickly gave up even writing my name on my brown bag. It felt silly and embarrassing to bother labeling such a meager package: "This lone apple belongs to Melissa. Keep out!" It seemed like an unnecessary precaution. What kid would pick up my bag and confuse it for their own, when theirs likely housed the heft and bulk of a fluffy white-bread sandwich stuffed with thick bologna slices and some mandarin orange wedges in light syrup in the plastic cup with its peel-back lid?

Then there were the hot-lunch kids, bused in from the fancy part of town. They could afford the forty-five-cent price tag for lunch every day. They got a new lunch card every Monday morning when they handed over their $2.25 to Edna, the head lunch lady, who made her rounds to all the classrooms and called out for all the hot-lunch kids to line up and get their new cards. That number for me was the magic value of wealth: having $2.25 to spend every single week on hot lunches. Hot-lunch kids didn't need loopy smiles on brown bags to know who they were; they had their names written in thick black ink by Edna. She was in charge of giving children identity and legitimacy via yellow cards that—as far as I was concerned—might as well have signified membership in an exclusive country club. The food we eat reinforces not just our ethnic or cultural identity but also our economic identity.

Sometimes I skipped lunch altogether. The charade of placing a small item in a bag and calling it lunch didn't seem worth it if I were running late. Or if I just felt lazy. Or if I were sick of apples. (To this day, I take issue with the dieting advice that "If you aren't hungry for an apple, then you aren't hungry." I *was* hungry—but not for an apple.) On these days I just floated around the cafeteria, hoping no one would notice that I was grazing Fritos and unwanted items other kids offered up before tossing in the garbage. Nonchalance is an attitude well practiced by a hungry child.

Feeding the Stomach and the Heart

One day everything changed. One of the hot-lunch kids noticed I wasn't eating and asked why I hadn't gone to the office. I'm sure I looked confused. He told me that if a student forgets lunch at home, the school had a policy of giving that student a lunch with an IOU that could be paid the next day. This information was shared in an earnest effort to help, but it was spoken with a casualness that could only come from knowing your family could afford to pay back the debt. I hesitated. I was not authorized to make forty-five-cent purchases without prior approval. I knew we could not pay the next day—and even if we could, we wouldn't because there was no way I would bring an IOU home to my mom and add to her stress.

I knew life was hard for her, and I did my nine-year-old best to protect her. Surely I was just being selfish, turning my nose up at tissue-paper meat and mealy, aged fruit, craving the hot, breaded mystery-meat fingers that hot-lunch kids ate, so absentmindedly swirling them in ketchup. But hunger is a deep need, far stronger than logic or feelings. Before I could lose my nerve to lie, I ran to the office and blurted out that I had forgotten my lunch. Within minutes, I was scarfing down the greasy, burnt-flour meat coating—a taste that was brand new, but whose aroma I recognized from years of eating apples down-wind from the hot-lunch table. I ate the fluffy little roll and the un-appealing canned peas that no other student ate, and I gulped it all down with chocolate milk. A drink? At lunch? Surely, I had arrived. I ignored the fact that I was lactose intolerant and never drank milk at home. Because, hello, *chocolate*? It tasted like a milkshake. And full felt better than anything else when I had to face afternoon fourth-grade math.

I started out forgetting my lunch once a week or so. I felt guilty eating food that I hadn't purchased, but eating a hot meal was too good. Soon, I was forgetting my lunch any time we were out of the pressed-pastrami product at home. And then even on days when I had a sandwich, I craved the comfort that only protein, fiber, fat, and vita-mins can give. I was hungry, and knowing food was feet away was enough to get me to lie once again to the school receptionist. The cycle sped up, and it became harder to leave it.

One day, however, the office monitor delivered a pink slip with my name on it: I was being called to the school office for principal-sized trouble. I smiled and shrugged to my classmates as I climbed out from my desk, acting as confused as they were about why a rule-following, good listener like me would be headed to the dreaded front office. But underneath my pretense of innocence, I knew: the jig was up. Luckily, I had a pressed meat and bread-heel sandwich with me that day. (Ah, the bread heel. Even today I avoid it when I pull bread from its package, slipping my fingers expertly under it to grab the softer, fluffier slices below. I was shocked to learn years later that my husband actually loves the heel, which is just one of the million ways I know we are meant for each other.)

On the short walk down the antiseptic-smelling, green-and-black pebbly-patterned school halls, I mentally reviewed all my options for addressing the debt, but I came up as empty as my stomach felt. The shame was crushing. *How had I become the kind of person who would steal food from the well-meaning school district?* I arrived at the principal's office timid and afraid, tears already filling my eyes. But the receptionist surprised me. She didn't mention my debt. And she didn't usher me in to see the principal. She just smiled and told me they were short-staffed in the cafeteria and were going to fill the slot with a student intern. That intern would help serve lunches to the kids and would get free lunch as payment. Would I be interested in the job? She made it seem like a business decision. No judgment. Just an option.

A job in food? I'd never dreamed of something so wonderful. Serving others and wearing a hairnet of my own sounded very grown-up. And I'd get to sit down to eat lunch while the other kids started recess.

I took the job. And though you might think I felt marginalized somehow, I didn't. I felt special. I got to know the lunch ladies because we served together and then we ate together, even Edna. They all adored me. They always let me pick my hairnet first, letting me have the pale brown ones to match my blonde hair, while they wore the black ones even though they clashed with their own puffy platinum hairdos. I started on the food line, serving a dinner roll or overly firm gelatin cubes ("finger jello," the menu called it) with a gloved hand, and I moved up quickly to hot-vegetable duty, where I was entrusted with an oversized metal spoon to scoop hot canned green beans or corn onto the compartmentalized plastic plates.

I became friendly with George, the jovial bald janitor who handed out milk cartons to the kids as they passed by the large metal cooler. On days that I gulped my milk down a little too quickly, George would sneak me a second little carton with a smile and a wink, before closing up the cooler and heading back to the business of emptying trash and sweeping floors. (In fifth grade, when our teachers announced one morning that George had suddenly died from a heart attack, no one else in my class seemed the tiniest bit concerned by the news, but I burst into tears, and I teared up for weeks whenever I reached out to collect the milk handed to me by his replacement.)

The receptionist, the lunch ladies, George, and Katy Rudder changed my life, and food was their main tool. Yet they did more than feed my body. They offered me compassion and made me feel valuable. By sharing God's provision with me, they reminded me that I was worthy of receiving his gifts, of food and of belonging. One small shift in degree can, over time, completely alter the trajectory of a path. Each of these kind people caused that one small shift in degree. How much of my academic success was due to their role in filling not only my stomach but also my heart? I'll never know. But I've been hungry in a classroom and I've been not hungry in a classroom, and every time I'd choose not hungry. I am kinder, more focused, more generous, more creative, and more grateful when both my body and my soul are nourished—when I feel fed and valued. I want that for everyone.

Food Unites

Food is one of God's great equalizers and unifiers. Everyone needs food to survive. Hunger hits us all the same. Without food, we realize quickly that we human beings are similar more than we're different. All of us also need God and his goodness and grace. Every meal we eat is a reminder of our shared dependence on God.

And every meal can be a reminder to share God's provision with others. Countless scriptural examples demonstrate our responsibility to share the earth's food. In Exodus, when the Israelites complained to God about their hunger as they were being delivered from Egyptian slavery, God offered them manna. This free food literally fell from the sky for people to pick up according to God's command to take only according to their need. No one was to hoard. When the people obeyed, "the one who gathered much did not have too much, and the one who gathered little did not have too little" (Exodus 16:18). Those with access were commanded to share the excess rather than assume privilege, and in fact if anyone did try to squirrel away extra manna for themselves, it became rotten and wormy and useless by morning. In the New Testament, Paul quoted this very verse from Exodus right after he declared, "The goal is equality" (2 Corinthians 8:14–15). This concept feels counter-cultural in today's system of consumer-goods allocation. But Jesus spent a lot of his time feeding the hungry. If you haven't read the book of Luke, I highly recommend it. Jesus ate his way through it, and he used food to equalize the marginalized and remind them—and everyone else—of their worth.

Jesus used food to break down the artificial, societal barriers we humans build. He fed the hungry, miraculously using small portions to serve many. And Jesus didn't just give food *to* the marginalized; he ate *with* them. It wasn't just what he gave but *who he sat with* to share a meal that unified. He welcomed the marginalized tax collector, the prostitute, the sinner, and the misfit to the table.

We might be tempted to donate money to a food bank and then cross our biblical calling to feed the poor off our spiritual to-do list. But that's not how Jesus worked. Katy Rudder didn't hand me a few corn chips and send me on my way. We shared a table . . . and our lives. Katy was the hands and feet of Jesus to me throughout my elementary school years.

Food, like a cafeteria, can unite us, or it can divide us. When I was hungry, I felt alone and isolated; I was one of the have-nots, unaware that others had also been dropped into the same bucket. When people shared with me and made sure I was fed, I felt their compassion and I felt community. I felt that I belonged. Turns out, this is a universal truth. Hunger and despair are inextricably linked, which is probably why Jesus talked about hunger and thirst so often. Through the actions of various people, God invited me into equality and unity—I felt both equal to the other kids who ate their meals and connected to them by our shared experience—and he invites us all. He used food to show me that I am a worthy part of this world, and I am a worthy part of him. In that elementary school cafeteria, God met me and invited me to be closer to him. Jesus is called the Bread of Life for good reason. While Jesus is our truest, deepest nourishment, our earthly food is a small experience of that deep eternal satisfaction. Meals in the modern world divide us sometimes more than unite us as they reflect socioeconomic and other divisions. But God's compassionate plan is for us to use food to unify and equalize instead.

RSVP to the Invitation into Compassion

- Jesus told us in Matthew 25:40 that how we treat others is how we are treating him: "Truly I tell you, whatever you did for one of the least of these brothers and sisters of mine, you did for me." Next time you walk or drive by someone in need, give them the honor and dignity of your eye contact. Try to see Jesus in their eyes. Even acknowledging someone's presence is honoring and validating.

- Ask your church if it has a food ministry or food access activities. Consider volunteering even for an event or two. Doing so may open your eyes to how you can be involved in making access to food equal for all.

- Equality begins when we connect outside of our normal social circles. Invite someone who is different from you—maybe you have different backgrounds, belief systems, or cultural histories—to share a meal.

- Find a local food-access program and spend a few minutes poking around on its website to learn about what it does. Click "volunteer" or "find out more" to learn about specific needs in your area and how you can be the hands and feet of Jesus in someone else's story.

Redeeming Loss with Food and Faith

An Invitation into Comfort

God can use food to remind us
that he is the ultimate redeemer.

Sharing our suffering builds deep communion—one that reminds us of our powerlessness as mortal humans; the strength and power of an all-knowing, loving God; and our calling to share one another's burdens. Food is a language of comfort for many of us. I don't mean eating a whole pizza to escape dealing with our hard stuff. I mean that food can draw us closer to others, which is probably why the meal train is the unofficial gesture we rely on to support someone in our community who is grieving or struggling. We don't always know how to say "I see your pain and I care," so we let the tuna-noodle casserole do some of the talking and make space for meaningful connection. God intentionally gave us people for relationship, and we are to "rejoice with those who rejoice; mourn with those who mourn" (Romans 12:15). Even in our darkest seasons, God can use food to nudge us closer to the people around us and to him. But I've gotten a little ahead of myself—sharing the good news before telling you about the grief. Since the sunshine is always more glorious after a cloudy day, I'll back up.

In contrast to my early childhood that was defined by lean times, striving for better times, and hope for the future, my teenage years felt like the glory days. Mom was finally a full-fledged doctor at the Bethesda Naval Hospital in the Washington, DC, suburbs, and the two of us—my sister had moved in with my dad when she was thirteen—moved into a sparkly new brick town house. We weren't wealthy by our neighborhood standards, but we felt rich! And we did all the things we could only dream of doing in the thrifty days of the past: we ate our morning cereal exclusively with half-and-half instead of milk, and we frequented restaurants without worrying (as much) about the check. Once we even bought Mom a new car on a whim because of the smell. For college, I purposely chose a school in New England where the ski-rack-and-Saab culture felt worlds away from my utility-room-bedroom in the small adobe house of my Arizona youth.

On April 13, 1989, I called my mom with a mundane and typical request for a college junior: I needed money. I wanted her credit card number so I could pay for a graduate school test-prep course. When her line was repeatedly busy, I got frustrated by that loud, obnoxious busy signal our generation would be the last to recognize.

For hours I called back, almost obsessively, dialing the numbers quickly in a pattern burned into my thumb's muscle memory. Just before giving up hope and going out for the night, the expected busy signal was replaced by a soft, purring ring—music to my ears. *Had I misdialed?* The line kept ringing, quietly and prettily. I was about to hang up and try again when an unfamiliar male voice answered curtly, and suddenly nothing was pretty. Instead of my mom waxing poetic about my future career in business while giving me her Amex number, the voice identified himself as a member of Maryland's Montgomery County police department. We had a very brief conversation that I can still recite word for word in my head. To this day, I have never repeated the conversation aloud, not even to my husband, but it has never left me. I learned from the officer that Mom had died by suicide.

She had been dead for a day. I had seen her the week before when I'd flown to DC from Vermont for a mother-daughter weekend. We'd spent the time together laughing, cooking, eating, watching movies, and shopping. We wandered the mall that whole Saturday, hunting for an outfit for my spring sorority formal. She'd bought me a dress more expensive than anything I'd ever owned—it cost four hundred dollars! Mom justified it happily over a late lunch by saying if I let her borrow it, it would be like each of us buying a two-hundred-dollar dress, and that seemed reasonable to her.

Mom was always an incredibly savvy shopper—early on because she had to be, and later probably more out of habit—and I inherited my love of budget hunting from her. But Mom could justify an expense when it suited her, usually when she wanted to separate herself from her past. I can still picture her sweet, conspiratorial wink over crab bisque at her favorite restaurant, Café La Ruche. We decided to buy that dress using her fuzzy calculations. When she died, I kept wondering, *Why would she kill herself when she'd planned to borrow that fancy dress? Her death ruined our math.* There is no accounting for what we focus on after a tragedy.

Her suicide shook the foundation of my life emotionally, financially, logistically, and spiritually. I was twenty years old. Her suicide didn't merely disrupt my life; it caused the very scaffolding of my existence to cave in. My sense of self was unanchored and thrown to the wind, and I sailed untethered for a long time afterward. I'm fortunate that I didn't veer permanently off course. But I spent an entire decade in deep grief, unable to make any sense of her death.

As a Christian, I couldn't figure out what it all meant for my mom. Was suicide an unforgivable sin? I didn't dare ask. I was too young, too scared, too naive to look it up. (This would later become an important lesson for me: don't be afraid to read the Bible to discover firsthand what God has to say.) If only I'd read the full New Testament, which says so clearly that we are saved by Jesus alone, not by our acts. Our works cannot earn us our salvation, erase our salvation, or separate us from God's unfathomable grace and love: "I am convinced that neither death nor life, neither angels nor demons, neither the present nor the future, nor any powers, neither height nor depth, nor anything else in all creation, will be able to separate us from the love of God that is in Christ Jesus our Lord" (Romans 8:38–39). I needed these words of the apostle Paul back then, but I didn't have them—only because I didn't look.

I don't believe my mom's suicide was ultimately a rejection of life. I think it was a horribly ineffective cry for more of the life that she felt she was supposed to be living. I imagine her being unable to put her finger quite on what the issue was, like an elusive itch she couldn't scratch. Still, my mom was an extraordinary woman whose end does not define her. Mom was funny, super smart, and beloved. Despite her personal chaos, Mom left behind in her death the gift of an anchor in an unfailing, very patient God. But it took me years to see that.

I wish I had leaned into God with my brokenness, and with my mom's. I wish I had trusted God with my struggles, because he could have handled it. Ten years is a long time to be in a spiritual winter. Ironically, the things that ultimately proved meaningless to my mom—career, money, success—became the things I sought all the more, almost as if I were trying to squeeze something out of them that she hadn't been able to. I finished college, put myself through business school, and created my own successful career, working in finance and strategy—first in consulting and then in corporate America. All of this served as my self-imposed quarantine from God. At least from most of him.

I clung to a tiny thread of hope, of knowing God was there in the background. I'd pray occasionally and attend church sporadically, as if God were a distant relative who needed updates in order to keep me in the will. But—I realized later—God patiently stayed close to me even though I didn't quiet down enough to hear him. Instead, I kept moving to the socially acceptable college-student rhythm: studying, dating, socializing, and partying away the grief. I made choices that I hope to guide my own daughters away from.

Grasping for the "Next Thing"

Although I had isolated myself in my spiritual vacuum, I wasn't alone in trying to make sense of Mom's suicide. Many of her friends and family wondered why, after so many difficult years, she would lose the will to live *after* she had arrived. Certainly Mom had had a tough life. She'd left an abusive home at the age of seventeen, taking a Greyhound bus across the country from New York to Tucson with exactly forty-two dollars in her pocket and an acceptance letter to the University of Arizona. There, she met a handsome fraternity boy named Jim Donovan. He had dreamy eyes, thick movie-star hair, and a kind, welcoming family. They married one weekend in Vegas at the Chapel of the Flowers. Their union lasted just long enough to produce my sister and, two years later, me. They divorced when I was a few months old. Mom was halfway through college, a single mom to two tiny blondes. She rose above the odds and tough financial times to put herself through college and medical school while raising her daughters alone. I was happy and doing well in college, with plans for graduate school on the horizon, and she'd finally achieved the successful career she had worked so hard to attain. So why would she intentionally end her life now? How did she keep her head up through so many difficult years only to be bowled over when she finally found success?

Even now, after nearly three decades to mull it over, I can still only guess. Suicide has complex root causes, and I'll never be able to get my arms fully around the state of Mom's mental health. But looking back, with the relative wisdom of hindsight, I can see clues that her soul felt unsettled. Her constant desire to move forward, become better, strive for more of everything—more success, more house, more money, more prestige, more social currency—kept her motivated in school, but I imagine that this relentless drive took its toll. Always wanting more, hunting for comfort or peace, never allows you to settle in and marinate in what's good about today even in its regular and imperfect normalcy. It took me years to figure out what my mom learned too late: wherever you go, you take you with you. This reality explains a little why Mom's big "arrival" was not only not enough to make her happy, but it might actually have been a source of huge disappointment as she discovered that widely celebrated success can't fix anything important.

We are inclined to think a magical Next Thing exists, which will make us happy in a long-term meaningful way: the promotion, a big break, a spouse, more money, a bigger or better home, a family. If I had to guess, Mom's Next Thing was so big that it kept her going for decades. If there is one gift I have taken from my mom's death, it is that I've learned to be content without always being happy. Sure, we get a mood spike when circumstances go our way, but true joy comes from feeling anchored and worthy, regardless of what is happening on the outside. That doesn't mean we don't feel sorrow or have rough days or weeks. But deep and abiding joy is big enough to house life's sorrows. We can feel incredibly sad and at the same time know we are abundantly loved and fundamentally okay. Joy isn't fleeting, and it can coexist with sorrow. In his letter to the Philippians, Paul said, "I know what it is to be in need, and I know what it is to have plenty. I have learned the secret of being content in any and every situation, whether well fed or hungry, whether living in plenty or in want. I can do all this through him who gives me strength" (4:12–13).

After all those years of living for the Next Thing, Mom finally became a successful physician. But I wonder if she was horribly let down to discover that the external stuff didn't change anything internal. The Next Thing (fill in the blank: money, boyfriend, new job, bigger house) can't fill that God-shaped hole in all of us. The good news is, I don't *need* a bigger house or a fancier car to be happy, and the essential news is that a bigger house and a fancier car *can't* make me—or you—happy long term.

Mental health is complicated, and I don't mean to oversimplify anyone's struggle. Most likely, Mom's lack of joy or hope was only one piece of an extremely complex puzzle. Which is just one reason why, as an advocate of mental wellness, I deeply wish we would do a better job of treating mental health issues and removing the stigma.

I understand the darker tendencies of my mom. I lived with her for a long time, and, more importantly, I share her DNA. I can feel when

I'm heading south to the border of mild depression. I know from experience when I need to fight the journey with copious amounts of self-care, eating well, sleeping well, exercising, and reaching out to loved ones to let them know I'm in a funk. I have learned from experience that I can keep myself from even starting the journey; I can keep my internal sense of well-being higher by staying connected—to God and to others—even when I feel like retreating and curling up into a ball. This explains why every study I've ever read about happiness points to one common denominator: connection. Do I dare suggest that connecting with God and people will make you fundamentally, at your core, happier in life? Yes, I do. I'd bet anything on it. Connection and comfort helped pull me from my spiritual winter, and that connection and comfort came through a vehicle that surprised me: food, and the people who shared it with me.

Healing Around the Table

When Mom died, leaving me with next to no money and life insurance policies made useless by suicide exclusions, my sorority sisters voted to let me live in the sorority house, rent-free, so I could be surrounded by their love. There wasn't even an empty bed at the time, so I slept on a couch in a bedroom already filled with three other girls. I'm sure I wasn't a convenient roommate to have, but sisterhood mattered more.

Living in the sorority house meant that instead of starting my mornings alone in an apartment and eating a quick bowl of cereal before trying to plow through both my grief and my day, I was nourished by a warm meal made by our longtime sorority cook, Linda, who was quick to give me a hug along with my plate of scrambled eggs. We would all sit at the huge dining room table in our pajamas and talk about everything that matters to the average college student: professors, classes, papers that were due, exams we had aced (or not), and who was dating whom. Linda's food kept us at the table long enough to open our hearts and share the small stuff in life, which gave us space to share the big stuff too. What an honorable task cooking dinner for others is! No matter what the day's schedule, and no matter how distracted by grief I might have felt in class, I knew that at 6:00 p.m. I'd be sitting with these women around this table, breaking bread and feeling a little bit like life was normal again. I even dared to start cooking my mom's favorite recipes myself, sharing the food with my friends.

Our housemother, Liz, kept tabs on me, and as we shared countless meals together, I could feel a closeness that hadn't been there before. She felt a strong sense of maternal obligation toward me, and I was grateful for it. Liz and I wrote letters for years, long after both of us left the university. And no one was more excited than Liz when I won *The Next Food Network Star.* I called Liz on her ninetieth birthday a few years ago, and even the sound of her voice took me right back to that soothing place around the Alpha Chi Omega table where my soul was cared for by the love of others. Liz died last year, but her legacy lives on through so many women, including me.

Liz, Linda, and my sorority sisters were only the beginning of the list of women who would become my community, who would love me through the isolation caused by my refusal to ask God any hard questions. When I was in graduate school in DC, I made friends with my classmates, and we shared our dreams and our lives over late-night BLTs and plates of over-easy eggs at the wonderfully dumpy all-night dive called the Tastee Diner. Those Formica tables with their tiny jukeboxes were the setting for hours of conversations that included my first glimpses into a future without Mom that didn't have me sobbing at the very thought. In my first post-MBA job, I worked for Andersen Consulting, designing financial services software, and became close to the only three other women in my recruiting class. Our friendship lines may have been drawn by our gender, but they were solidified by our love for the amazing food available in Washington, DC. As we sampled all the tiny ethnic restaurants that were the secret gems of the city, we shared our lives bite by bite. One of those women later gifted me my very first study Bible, and I still use it today.

The amount of life that is shared while eating is truly extraordinary, and every one of those moments is a gift from God. Ten years of these connections with people piled up and comforted me. God was patiently, gently nudging me. I am reminded of the sick boy's father who cried out to Jesus: "I do believe; help me overcome my unbelief!" (Mark 9:24). Those ten years helped my unbelief. When I settled into my thirties, I finally realized that God had been with me all along, even when I hadn't felt him. So if you've ever felt distant from God, even for a decade (or more!), the good news for all of us is that God's presence in our lives is not to be confirmed by our ability to feel him with us. Knowing that truth gets me through the moments of doubt and isolation that sometime creep into my life.

Redeeming the Day

Mom's death certificate says April 12. The police report and tombstone say April 13. So I get to commemorate her death over two days every year. I wish I had decided early on just to pick a date and stick with it instead of letting the anniversary linger over forty-eight difficult hours when I would feel the void where my mom's wisdom, warmth, and laughter should be. For years, April 12 and 13 always felt dark and empty.

One year, though, something changed. Philippe and I were eager to start a family from the moment we were married in 2003. Some medical issues related to my fertility concerned my doctor, so from the start I charted my cycles and took regular blood tests. For green-card reasons, Philippe and I had to be apart. I worked in Los Angeles, and he, awaiting his paperwork, worked in Paris. We spent all of our free time and money hopping on planes back and forth between LA and Paris. Our carefully timed trysts, which were sometimes honeymoon-awesome but sometimes admittedly perfunctory, were always followed by deep sorrow when my period continued to arrive like clockwork. Longing, then hope followed by heartbreak, became the rhythm of our newlywed year. It was exhausting, physically and emotionally. Every month I wept, worried that after losing my mother, I seemed unable to create my own family. My doctor felt like it might be time to consider other options.

Much prayer led me to the comforting idea that perhaps Philippe and I were meant to adopt. God creates families in so many wonderful and unexpected ways, and I came to feel in my heart that adoption was far more than a plan B—it might be my own beautiful plan A. But just as we began investigating the next steps, we got the surprise of two blue lines: I was pregnant. It was early May 2004. I raced to Philippe, still sound asleep, waving the little pee-stick in my hand, my pajamas tangled around my ankles, tripping me. Later that week, I met with our doctor, and he told me what I could already see clearly on my ovulation chart: I had gotten pregnant sometime between April 12 and April 13. Somehow we created a little someone on the perfect two days—the very dates that had haunted me for so many years. That knowledge healed something in me. I felt as if we had filled in a tiny bit of the black hole left by Mom's too-soon departure.

The following year, when April 12 and 13 arrived, I longed for that feeling of healing again. If I could create something and deliberately contribute to the world in a positive way, I could heal a little more each year. Making a baby every April seemed unsustainable, so I turned to the creation that spoke to me most: food. I made a pan of brownies. On a whim, I gave them to a neighbor who happened to stop by. So I made some more for us—and then a third pan for Philippe's classmates at graduate school. Each brownie square I cut filled me with purpose and healing. The following year, I made brownies again, this time for our new neighbors in Texas. And my two days of creation were born. Every year, I find comfort in creating. Some years I celebrate April 12 and 13 with a small gesture, delivering a baked good to a neighbor. Sometimes, on those days that quietly commemorate Mom, I don't even mention the dates to anyone and simply serve my family Mom's flank steak recipe (her fanciest one!) or her Israeli nut torte, which is a somewhat dry, dense cake made of ground walnuts.

One year, I was booked to speak at a suicide-prevention fund-raiser on my mom's anniversary, so I couldn't be in the kitchen. When the foundation sent me the plane ticket to the East Coast, I noticed that my flight was scheduled to leave California on the afternoon of April 12 and that I would arrive just after midnight—in the early hours of April 13. I had to smile because even though I wasn't cooking anything, I was still creating by being part of the fund-raiser. Scripture tells us that all things work together for the good of those who love the Lord (Romans 8:28). There is beauty and harmony in life if only we look for it.

Food, and the people connected to that food, played a big part in the long healing of my grief. Today I'm older than my mom ever was, which feels weird. So how do I reconcile her death now? First, I live with purpose and joy. I find my identity, including my work identity, in God. Genesis tells me that I was made in God's image, and Jesus tells me that I am renewed in him. I define success differently and have come to believe in the depths of my gut that joy truly is an inside job. Second, I honor my mom by raising four young women with care, purpose, heart, and humility. What a privilege that I get to be their mentor along their journeys to womanhood! I also stay connected—through relationships, prayer, and food. Every single day, I get to make food for my family, share food with friends, and write recipes for people I've never even met. Every day I get to create and contribute to the world. By doing so, I hope to shine a small light not just on the beauty of creation but also on the Creator himself. Food truly has been an incredibly healing force since losing Mom—from the hundreds of meals I've shared with loyal friends to the plates of brownies I give to neighbors. In all this, I've seen God's grace and redemption.

If you feel as if you are missing the redemption, keep going. The comfort will come. Sometimes the only way out of a spiritual winter is to go through it. But God is there, I am sure of it. Feel free to borrow my faith on this one if you want.

RSVP to the Invitation into Comfort

- List your big Next Things. Sometimes they masquerade as dreams and hopes. Ask yourself if you are living today as if you will be fundamentally happier once the Next Thing arrives. Is there anything you might be putting off until that Next Thing comes? Consider what it might be like to hold those dreams

a little more loosely, still pursuing them with vigor,
but choosing to embrace life and be grateful for
today exactly the way it is.

- Jesus used a food metaphor to talk about the need
for death before redemption: "Very truly I tell you,
unless a kernel of wheat falls to the ground and dies,
it remains only a single seed. But if it dies, it produces many seeds" (John 12:24). Grab a slice of
bread or a cracker and take a tiny bite. Slowly savor
the taste and consider the death of the seed that was
redeemed in the tasty cracker. In what ways does
that bring you comfort and inspire you?

- If you are struggling or know someone who might
be struggling with thoughts of suicide, connect with
the American Foundation for Suicide Prevention
online at AFSP.org or reach out to the suicide
hotline 1-800-273-TALK.

Chapter 3

Finding God in Culinary Chaos

An Invitation into Creation

God is the Creator of all,
and we can create, too.

B eing on Food Network brought me closer to God. Even making the video to audition for *The Next Food Network Star* awakened the realization in me that I was made in his image and hardwired to create. But the story starts long before then.

In fact, it goes all the way back to Genesis. The very first sentence of the Bible says, "In the beginning God created." He is our Creator. He created light, darkness, water, sky, plants, animals, and humans. I can imagine God, with the artistic joy of a young child building an entire world out of modeling clay, gleefully and carefully choosing every detail, and then stepping back to evaluate his work. And God called the whole creation "very good." God loves to create! And he crafted us with the ability to create too.

I imagine he wants us to use our unique talents and gifts to make our own mark in the world, adding to its beauty and worth as best we can. I create recipes that reflect my wonder in delightful tastes and provide nutrition for my family and fans. Before that, for many years I was a finance executive, which has its own kind of creativity, but God used food to tap into the deepest, most authentic creator in me, and that drew me closer to him—which I needed because my life was filled with hunger and want.

Before Mom died, I'd had big dreams of practicing business law: I would earn an MBA and JD and then crush the world of mergers and acquisitions contracts, all while wearing sleek and fashionable suits. I was accepted into graduate school and planned to attend, even though my emotional well-being, let alone career aspirations, hung by a thread in the darkness of my grief.

A year might sound like a long time, but the one-year anniversary of my mom's death had me feeling as though time had betrayed me: How could she have already died "a year ago"? My college graduation sneaked up on me just weeks after the first anniversary of losing Mom, and the thought of facing what should be a happy day put dread in my belly. The campus would soon be crawling with happy graduates and their very-alive moms and families, posing for the camera, eyes bright with hope for the future. No one would be there for me. It was just too much.

To avoid a heartbreaking day, I probably made a major decision too quickly: I skipped graduation, wrote a letter to the graduate school whose offer I had accepted and unaccepted it, and moved to Greece to work on a cruise ship. *A year away from life as I knew it to call bingo and sing in shows on a ship was just the trick to avoid facing graduation day alone,* I told myself. Plus, the one-way ticket to Athens promised an adrenaline rush that would push back the loneliness. At least for a little while.

Eventually, my travel year as "Julie McCoy" came to an end, and I hung up my name tag and returned to the States to attend graduate school in Washington, DC. Georgetown's MBA program cost a private-school fortune, so to help cover expenses, I took my first paying food job. I worked as a live-in cook for a large, eccentric family, all of whom oddly spoke with the slightest British accent despite being 100 percent American.

My job was to provide three nourishing meals a day for a large family—and it was harder than Alice from *The Brady Bunch* (my only mentor in this space) had led me to believe. Every morning I packed school lunches for the kids and delivered a to-go breakfast and thermos of coffee to the front seat of the mom's car, along with her keys (placed in the ignition). And each evening I served the family a sit-down dinner.

I didn't know what I was doing, but I took the job seriously to compensate for my lack of experience. I managed the weekly menu using a Lotus 1-2-3 spreadsheet (which, if you're too young to remember, is what we had before Excel). I brainstormed meals and tweaks for the picky kiddos. I managed all the groceries, too, filling a supermarket cart nearly full with gallons of milk alone, a glimpse into what grocery shopping would eventually look like for me years later as the mom in my own big family. At the local farmers market, I gathered sumptuous in-season produce. Yellow squash and zucchini might inspire a summer vegetable soup. Ripe peaches and raspberries ended up in a cobbler. While not glamourous, the job was creative and satisfying, even if fitting it in between a full-time course load and homework made me feel like I was either cooking or studying 24-7.

I wasn't the only help in the house. A gardener named Betty and I each had a small bedroom in the attic. Betty had a day job as an attorney and moonlighted for this quirky family. Why a lawyer moonlighted as a live-in gardener never became clear to me, but I was glad for both the company and her solid gardening skills. Thanks to Betty, the backyard offered lots of fodder for delicious meals. She grew luscious tomatoes and copious amounts of basil, which I gathered to make endless batches of homemade tomato sauce.

Eyeing one of my many pots of simmering sauce one evening, my boss looked at me from behind his newspaper and giant tumbler of Drambuie—a sweet, whiskey-based liqueur of which he drank a half bottle nightly. "Melissa," he said, with his nose tipped down so he could make eye contact over his reading glasses, "don't think for one minute that this family is above a *lasagna*." He emphasized the word *lasagna,* and his accent went from British to slightly Italian. Sure, I had grown up on food stamps, but until that moment it had never occurred to me that even the wealthiest people might deem something so delicious as cheesy pasta goodness beneath them. But then again I'd never heard Americans speak with a British accent. I wasn't sure if he was joking, but he seemed earnestly curious to dabble in what he considered a peasant pasta dish. So I created my first recipe for a lasagna that night, hoping that by adding a creamy béchamel sauce, I'd be making the dish a little fancier, just in case I'd read him wrong.

After a semester of trying to balance being a live-in cook and studying, I decided to double down on student loans and find a more flexible job. But despite the craziness of the work (and the household Drambuie consumption), I had no regrets: I had experienced my first true food job, and, to my delight, I had become a cook.

I kept cooking for myself and my roommates throughout grad school, becoming famous for my many rice-and-bean slow-cooker creations that could feed a crowd for less than five bucks. After earning my

MBA, I worked in corporate finance, so my budget loosened, and I began to cook more often for my friends. I hosted dinner parties and became a cookbook junkie. I had a library of cookbooks with strips of paper marking recipes I couldn't wait to try. I'd tweak an occasional ingredient here and there, but I knew in my gut that I was a student, so I followed recipes to the letter, learning the rhythm and cadence of a well-constructed dish. I was adventurous in my personal cooking, but when I had guests, I relied on tried-and-true recipes I knew I could execute. If the nineties had an official meal for me, it would be my go-to company dinner: chicken marbella from my old standby cookbook, *The Silver Palate*. It was a simple dish that delivered big on flavor and taught me about balancing sweetness, acidity, bitterness, and saltiness. The recipe was based on marinating the chicken overnight in a perfect marriage of herbs, brown sugar, prunes, olives, capers, and white wine, and tasty results were guaranteed. Making chicken marbella so many times gave me the confidence to branch out the tiniest bit on my own: I swapped out the brown sugar for honey, for instance. I know this doesn't scream "future Food Network star," but I share this as a reminder that everyone starts at the beginning. These early years were the start of my becoming more creative with food.

Learning a Way to Cook

In 2000, after several years working for Disney at its headquarters in Burbank, I moved to Paris for a job leading the merchandise finance team for Disneyland Paris boutiques and outlets. I also helped create the boutiques for their second theme park, Disney Studios. I was thrilled to move to Paris, but when I saw the size of the moving crate the company sent for overseas shipment, my heart sank. I had to fit my entire life into a few cubic feet plus what I could pack in my suitcase. My cookbooks stayed behind. And while that sounds like not a big deal today, back then—without ebooks or a reliable, speedy internet—this loss was devastating. Searching for dinner ideas or pulling up my favorite white chicken chili recipe online wasn't an option.

Still, I was determined to be open to my new Parisian life and to adopt a beginner's mind. I am an optimist by nature. Even though I could barely speak enough French to order lunch in a restaurant, I imagined that I would be charming with my American accent. I pictured ending each day by walking home from the Métro with a beret on my head and a baguette tucked under my arm.

In reality, my life in France was nothing like my dreams. Moving to a foreign country alone was far more difficult than the phrase *I'm moving to Paris!* ever let on. I missed everything that tethered me and made me feel at home. I felt overwhelmed and completely lost. I ate cornflakes for breakfast—they were one of the few products on the French shelves that I recognized from my home—and I cried salty tears into the bowl almost every morning. Then I splashed cold water on my face and pulled myself together just in time to run to the smelly Métro station and catch the last possible train that would get me to work on time. (I later referred to the first half of this year in France as my crying-in-my-cornflakes days because that's what I remembered most about those hard, lonely months.)

If ever I needed the comfort of a familiar meal pulled from the dog-eared pages of my well-loved cookbooks, it was then. But it's funny how God works in those spaces of emptiness and weakness. When we release our grip on an identity that we've clung to, God can do so much, and we can finally hear about his plan for us because we aren't too busy being fabulous to stop and listen. Sometimes, when we feel as if life is all falling apart, it's actually all falling together.

Anyway, it should be no surprise that food was at the heart of my Paris recovery from misery. The language of food is universal, and besides, as I have mentioned, ordering in French was already squarely in my skill set. (*Un café au lait, s'il vous plaît!* I mean, what could go wrong?) But here is the secret to getting connected in Paris if your French is iffy: food shops are the one place in Paris where shop owners aren't in a hurry. They couldn't wait to share their expertise and didn't mind repeating themselves slowly for my American ear. In those shops I found my voice and my smile and the space to be me even though I was stumbling my way through another language. Perhaps the stumbling was exactly the thing I needed to slow me down long enough to truly appreciate the ingredients and food. When I was in Paris, I also realized it was time to branch out from the safety of familiar cookbook recipes and find new ways to prepare food. I doubt I would have been brave enough to do this unless life circumstances had made me.

Fortunately, I was in the center of the food world. And it was there in Paris that I fell in love with food. I gathered ingredients from small, specialized stores curated by true experts in their field. I bought cheese from a purveyor who sold nothing else, and I bought produce at a place called Palais des Fruits ("Fruit Palace"). My fish came from a fishmonger's shop and my meat from the chilled, bright-white counters of the local butcher. At the Italian market I found homemade pastas, and I popped into the bakery daily for fresh bread. I shed my rigid notions of what recipes called for—mostly because my recipes were thousands of miles away—and began instead to purchase food that most appealed to me and then I created meals from those ingredients.

For me, Paris definitely wasn't always the romantic city I saw in the movies. Sometimes it was polluted, smelly, rude, and busy—and trying to settle there was hard. But Paris is where I found God in ingredients. His glory shone in the turnips, fresh from the earth, their errant roots untrimmed and soil clinging to them. Full chickens, heads and feet still attached, hung from hooks in the butcher shop. I was accustomed to sanitized, plastic-wrapped packages that spoke more of man's impact on this earth than God's creation of it. But God leaves his fingerprints on the food he has given us, though I was used to seeing no trace of them in my American upbringing.

In Paris, food was different, and I was different too. My office had always been where I felt valued and powerful. In Paris, I was surprised to discover that at work I felt broken and weary, lost in the language and culture differences. I was no longer the sassy corporate-ladder climber I had become in Los Angeles. But with nothing to lose and no friends to speak of in my new life, I walked bravely into the butcher shop and bought meat hanging from a hook. At the time I thought I was toughening up, courageously selecting the chicken whose life once as a breathing, walking animal on a farm was now over. But, in fact, I was softening as a realization of God's creation washed over me and infused me with deeper appreciation of the life my food had before it hit my table.

Food shops became my own little respite. I bought my baguettes from the bakery below my apartment. The bakery's aromas would waft upward starting in the wee hours of the morning, and I'd eat the bread knowing it had been truly a labor of love performed by people who knew my name and welcomed my daily visits. Buying cheese, I'd pause long enough to hear the *fromagier's* stories of its history, and although I couldn't understand it all, I learned that even cheeses have natural seasons that the French respect, an idea that shocked this American who was used to grabbing any kind of cheese at any time of the year.

These ingredients—these godly works of art—inspired my cooking and soothed my frayed soul. It was as if God started planning supper, and then I showed up to the kitchen midproject: some vegetables yet unwashed, the meat still wrapped in white paper, the utensils strewn about on the counter—messy evidence of creation. But I got to pick up the ingredients and continue the creation God began, without a cookbook and without any expectations because during those first few months I lived in France, I didn't have any friends who needed to be fed. In those early days, only God and I were at the table. I learned to trust both his ingredients and my ability to honor them.

Have you ever watched *Top Chef*? (Of course you have. You are only human.) For me, Paris was a little like the *Top Chef* challenges in which one contestant starts cooking a dish and then another chef rotates in and must continue the dish without consulting the person who started it. The chefs gather clues about the dish they are cooking; they look at it, smell it, and taste it to figure out what has been created so they can continue the creation. It's the same with God, the ultimate Creator: his work leaves clues. In Paris, I began to look for his clues and continue his good work. I bought unfamiliar greens and turned them into salads. I selected less common cuts of meat, like the duck neck or beef shoulder, and prepared them according to the butcher's suggestions, using my newly informed judgment, not a recipe, to decide what ingredients to add and when the dish was done.

I leaned into the French food culture even more when I started dating a nice French man named Philippe, who at that time didn't speak a word of English, which meant we spoke only in French for our first several years together. He introduced me to the best quirky Parisian restaurants far off the touristy paths. One time we ate cheese cured in maggots, which I disliked, but not as much as you might expect. We became regulars at a restaurant in the Chinese quarter of Paris—where my tiny apartment was—because it was open late (I would often take the late train home from work, so we would eat dinner at eleven o'clock or midnight). On weekends I would cook dinners for Philippe, most commonly a simple ingredient-inspired, no-recipe dish that was the precursor to the four-step chicken I made on the finale of *The Next Food Network Star*.

We married a few years later in Philippe's village in the South of France and moved back to the United States for Philippe to attend graduate school at Northwestern University, which is, incidentally, what motivated Philippe to finally learn English. Dropping both of our salaries to move to Chicago, where one of us would attend a very expensive graduate school, of course, meant it was an excellent time to start a family. We had Valentine in Philippe's first year of school and Charlotte in his second year. After his MBA graduation, we moved to Texas for his job. That year we had our twins, Margaux and Océane—when Valentine was two and Charlotte was one. Sidenote: four kids in diapers is no joke. Phew. (Sidenote update to the sidenote: four teenage girls is perhaps even less of a joke. Yikes.)

Within just a few years, we had transitioned from two incomes and no kids, living the social, urban Parisian life, to one income and four kids in suburban Dallas. I relied on my finance background and became strategic about our household budget. If I could find millions of dollars of savings in the Disney budget, then certainly I could find ten dollars in our own! I put my energy into managing our household budget and shared my creative money-saving tips with my fellow mom friends.

While I was a stay-at-home mom to our babies, I started speaking to local mom groups about my guerrilla money-saving techniques, some in the kitchen, some not. The topic that most interested every audience I visited was how I saved more than a hundred dollars a month by making my own yogurt without any special equipment in my hot Texas garage.

We needed to save that extra money, but what I loved about making yogurt was getting to be creative with the ingredients, turning inexpensive milk into creamy yogurt that all six members of my family loved. As for the process, I'd feel for the right temperature with my fingertips, wrap the jars of warm milk in blankets, and then settle them into their rest in the toasty garage. I felt like I was in Paris again, cooking with God's ingredients. I started hosting people in my home to show them my tips and tricks. Word spread, and finally I had too many women to keep up with the yogurt-making demand—I still had four babies to manage—so I made a video. That video, which I recorded in one quick take while my babies were all napping one day, is the video I submitted to Food Network, and it led to me being cast on the fifth season of *The Next Food Network Star*.

Trusting the Creator in Me

Nearly a decade after I'd arrived in France and discovered my love of food and how God was connected to the ingredients, I arrived on the set of *The Next Food Network Star*, having no idea that I was in for a continuation of those lessons I learned in Paris. Back then, the show followed the classic reality show format, where life in "the house" was a big part of the episodes. We were mic'd and filmed much of the day, even outside the cooking challenges. The first thing filmed was each contestant arriving at the house, meeting the other competitors, answering questions about their backgrounds, and appearing to look interested.

But as later on-camera interviews confirmed, we were primarily sizing up our competition: How good were the other chefs? And how many safe weeks did we have before the real competition kicked in?

I had watched enough reality television (or "documentaries," as I like to call them) to know what I was getting myself into. Reality shows cast certain archetypes. There's the handsome young man with more spunk than experience juxtaposed with the wiser, older character. There's almost always an over-the-top-but-hilarious-and-often-gay guy, and there's always a cute blonde. Standard casting moves.

As I went into this first day of filming, I promise you that I truly thought I was that blonde. Never mind that I had just birthed four children in two and a half years years and was sporting a really unfortunate haircut. Or that I was already forty years old—and not Jennifer Aniston forty, but real-life forty. When the cameras started rolling, the set quieted, and I heard the word *action* for the first time, and then I walked into the house and met my fellow contestants. I realized immediately there was definitely a gorgeous blonde on the show. And it wasn't me. That didn't bother me, actually—being "the blonde" felt like a misconception to have to shake—but it left me wondering: *What piece of the casting puzzle am I?*

A few hours into filming, I figured it out: I was the well-meaning but underqualified suburban housewife from Texas. I would be the kindhearted mom of four kiddos in diapers, bumbling around in a commercial kitchen for the first time. All of this was technically true, but from my perspective, these were all merely elements of my life experience, not the entirety of who I was. It never occurred to me that I would be defined this way, both by the viewers and by my fellow contestants. In a casual conversation during one of our many van rides to a challenge, I mentioned having visited Thailand before moving to Paris for my job with Disney. You'd have thought I said I'd traveled to the moon. The other contestants were shocked that this suburban, diaper-bag-carrying mom had traveled beyond the borders of Costco and Babies "R" Us. That I had an MBA and a prebaby, decadelong career in finance was another mindblower.

On that first morning we headed to the Food Network Kitchen, where we met the judges and stood shoulder to shoulder in a lineup while the cameras captured them sizing us up in awkward silence. Glancing out of the corners of my eyes, I glimpsed a huge commercial kitchen that looked nothing like mine at home, and the contestants included incredibly talented individuals—one was the official cook for a major league sports team and another had opened thirty restaurants across the country. I was more than a little overwhelmed. I felt sure I would be the first elimination. Maybe I was just a token baby bottom–wiping addition to the show.

We received our first challenge right away: make a dish for a large party celebrating Food Network's sweet sixteen. I made mini apple tarts with a butter crust that my mother-in-law had taught me the first year Philippe and I were together. I'd never made pie (or anything) for a hundred people before. I multiplied my pastry recipe in my head and hoped for the best. As I carefully counted the many cups of flour and poured them into the gigantic Food Network food processor, Bobby Flay stopped by my station to chat, per standard reality-cooking-TV-show operating procedure: "What are you making? Are you afraid you might not have enough time? I'll leave you to it!" This was the first time I'd ever spoken to him, unless you count the time only a few months earlier when I stood in line for hours at Williams-Sonoma to get his autograph on his cookbook, and I'd had zero chill. (I still have that photo of our first meeting—adoring fan and television star!) And

I had zero chill now, meeting Bobby again while I was cooking on his show.

Were my hands even moving and adding flour to the monster-sized food processor as he spoke to me? I had no idea. I'd completely lost track of where I was in my recipe, which in baking spells catastrophe. When Bobby walked away, I looked at the mound of flour and butter and had no idea about how much of what I needed next. I had a moment of reckoning: *Was I going to fall apart and go under? Prove the fellow contestants (and my fears) right, that I didn't belong there? That a mom's voice didn't belong in the bigger food conversation? Or was I going to rise to the occasion and make my point of view—shaped by my humble beginnings, a love for ingredients, and my penchant for saving money—part of the food landscape?* The answer was in the bowl of the food processor: focus on the food, the ingredients. And that answer was from the same God who had shown himself in the ingredients every time I cooked. Let the baking ratios guide me—sure, especially in baking—but rely on the food itself to tell me what it needed to shine. I dug my hands into that dough (I removed the blade—safety first!) and felt my way through, deciding if it needed a little more flour or butter. I was, after all, a creator, and touching the dough connected me back to my Creator.

I created tarts for a hundred people, and Bobby and Giada praised the pastries as one of the best dishes of the night. I was elated to make it to a second week, but more than that, I was relieved to have found my footing in something solid: God. This served me throughout the entire seven weeks of filming.

"Trust the ingredients" became my mantra.

The whole experience of *The Next Food Network Star* was surreal. All the women slept in creaky bunk beds in one room. Night after night, I lay there listening to the unfamiliar breathing and snoring of strangers, of my competitors. *When will the staff wake us and what will our day be like? Will it be a crazy-long day involving hours of van travel? Or will we have a relatively easy "interview" day or a shorter challenge right there in the Food Network Kitchen?* Not knowing how long the day would be, when it would start, what we would be eating, or if someone was going to be sent home that day was destabilizing. I constantly felt short of information that could provide a sense of context and allow me to relax. Going to bed at night, bone tired from a stressful day of cooking or a nerve-wracking, five-hour elimination session disoriented us constantly. Pushed into a corner, feeling less than adequate compared to the impressive chef's résumés of most of the competitors, and unable to rely on my normal life skills to cope, I—and everyone else—was forced to find my own steady ground.

I found God to be my rock; reliable in a strange, unpredictable world. I wrote prayers of gratitude to him at night, and during the day I fought my nerves by attempting to find him in the food displayed on tables for us by the Food Network culinary department. I focused hard on the God who created the greens that sat there unassuming and ready to be transformed by a food challenge. I was deliberate about finding God through the food I made each day with nothing but his ingredients to inspire me—no recipes, no slips of paper, no internet, not even a magazine or book to read at night. The food is what got me through, the food is what invited me to create, and the food is what settled me and made me feel okay and worthy of my point of view when compared against the fancy plating and swooshes from chefs using ingredients I'd never seen sold in a Safeway. I adjusted to the emotional rhythms, clung to God, and I finally stopped trying to guess what was ahead.

To be clear, I had known what I was signing up for. Watching the group of "cheftestants" get wide eyed at the surprise of an unexpected crazy challenge is part of the appeal of a cooking competition; it makes for good television. But painting a picture of this reality-TV world we were living in helps explain why the ingredients became my tether connecting me back to God. I wouldn't have any idea in advance of what the challenge would be, nor could I predict if I would be well rested, well fed, and well prepared, but I knew I would have access to a carefully organized pantry of ingredients, and I knew who had made them. I trusted God's ingredients and who the creator God had made me to be, so I felt confident that I could respond to the challenge.

The contestants and I would stand in a line, while one of the judges announced the challenge: "A brand-new burger for Bobby Flay's restaurant!" Or "A regional dish—using an assigned ingredient basket—for military heroes!" To shut off the mounting stress, I would remind myself that once I got to the ingredients, I would be okay.

Just get to the ingredients, because God is there, I told myself. As I learned to trust that God would fill my creator's well abundantly, the fear of running out of ideas subsided. Trusting the creator in me was one of the greatest gifts I received from being on *The Next Food Network Star.*

As I grew used to the unnatural rhythms of *The Next Food Network Star* life for seven weeks, I noticed a shift. I started running to the ingredients, to grab God's gift and then glorify him. Once I got to the food, the cameras slipped away from my focus, and the challenge was no longer between me and the other chefs, and it was no longer about being watched by thousands of viewers. The challenge was now a partnership: I felt as if God and I were creating together. Creating and living and working not just *for* God but *with* him. I cooked with God alongside me, and I cooked for this audience of one.

Being on *The Next Food Network Star* was noisy business, so much so that I had to make a decision. Would I worry about the cameras, the competition, how I looked on television, and potential elimination, and try to control the uncontrollable? *Or* would I focus deep and hard on God and on who he had made me to be? I found peace and stability in the latter. God is always the right place for me to fix my eyes, but it took a wild (media) storm around me and his calming, creative presence through food during a reality-TV competition for me to embrace that truth fully. Winning the competition wasn't so much the prize as the by-product of the real win: finding my center in God.

Working on my own cooking show put me less in the role of shiny television star and more in the role of creator in a big way: I was developing hundreds of recipes to make on *Ten Dollar Dinners,* as well as creating food for talk shows like the *Today* show and *The Rachael Ray Show,* writing cookbooks, and creating new recipes each week for my Associated Press column. My job became literally creating something—a recipe—that didn't exist before. The sheer volume of the recipes I needed to develop felt daunting at first. I would stand in my kitchen, staring at a counter filled with ingredients, and I realized that I was revisiting *The Next Food Network Star* competition and that I could also revisit my dependence on the food and on the God who made it.

To some it may seem I am just creating recipes, but I've come to think of it as holy work. Through recipes, I have a chance to be a part of the meals of thousands of families. In a small way, my fingerprints are in the homes of people I will never meet. Recipe writing is one way I connect with others. When a woman stops me on the street (or more likely at Costco when I'm wearing a ponytail and no makeup, which guarantees she will ask for a photo) to tell me she made my

potato-bacon torte, I want to stop shopping and talk about her experience. I want to sit with this person, have coffee, and ask her about her
family, and the day she made the recipe, and how it made her feel. I
want to tell her the story of why I made the recipe in the first place,
and I want to compare notes and share life, and a hug, and maybe
even some tears of sisterhood over potato pie. Is that too much to ask
of a list of ingredients and instructions? Not if it's God's work, I don't
think. The God I know is capable of doing big things through the
small stuff.

It took *The Next Food Network Star* and a barrage of recipe writing
to make me appreciate the holiness of the recipe-driven tasks in front of
me. The program also shed new light on the cooking I had done all
along, even back in graduate school. Home cooking, my friend, is also
holy. In fact, perhaps it is even more deeply so. While a recipe I write
can reach thousands, it will admittedly touch them in a cursory, shal-
low way. I doubt anyone who grabs a chicken piccata recipe from my
website is going to pause as they print it and shout, "Hallelujah, I feel
the Lord here!" (Although, feel free.) No, recipe ministry is far more
subtle. But home cooking is a chance to touch those around our tables
directly and deeply. That sheet-pan salmon you make every Friday is
more than just dinner; it's a continuation of what the Lord started.

We Are All Creators

Why did God make us creators? God gives us what he holds dear—
what he himself treasures. He made us creators out of his love for us. In
Isaiah 43:7, he says that we were created for his glory. God gave us ingredients and the ability to think, to work, and to build so that we
would create as he did. God set up an easel and loaded it up with can-

vases, brushes, and richly colored paints, and he waits on the sidelines, watching us create. The bounty of ingredients he provides is astounding. We are meant to use them to create with and to bring God glory. I don't mean we have to cook every day, all the time, or that we need to make it our profession. But when we create something with nature's ingredients, we are drawn closer to God, even if it's just to make a simple supper for our families on a Tuesday night.

In the dark first years of grieving my mom's suicide, I was awakened to the joy of food through the quirky family who hired me to cook for them. Then in the loneliness and fear of moving to a new country, I found God in small food shops and my tiny Parisian kitchen. And in the dizzying world of reality television, I anchored myself to God and held on tight for the crazy ride.

Our creative activity—cooking and otherwise—is one way we thank God for the raw material. Creating will bring us closer to God, both because it pleases him and because we get to emulate God in Genesis. Anytime we create—anytime we do something that adds value to our earth—we get a tiny glimpse into what God was doing in early Genesis. What I wish I could go back and tell my twenty-something self is that even my job in "noncreative" finance had creation at its center. I've always been a creator and didn't know it. So have you.

RSVP to the Invitation into Creation

- The first words of the Bible tell us God is a creator: "In the beginning God created the heavens and the earth" (Genesis 1:1). Later, in verse 27, we read, "God created mankind in his own image." Consider taking inspiration from Genesis and reframing your

work in the kitchen as creation and worship. Invite
God into the kitchen to cook with you, and think of
yourself as finishing his masterpiece. (Put on a little
praise music—or Beyoncé—if you want!)

- Set your alarm early and be one of the first to arrive
at a farmers market just to browse. Talk to the
farmers and vendors about their food and how they
like to prepare it. (Tip: you may want to take a little
cash and a canvas tote in case you get inspired!)

- Have a repertoire of a few recipes that you can make
with confidence. They don't have to be complicated!
You'll be surprised how empowering it is to have a
few simple meals you can easily throw together.
Once you've mastered those recipes, try tweaking
them to make them your own.

Chapter 4

Letting Go and Leaving the Results to God

An Invitation into Authenticity

God has the long view, and we can trust
him with the results, giving us permission
to drop our masks and show up for life,
embracing our true selves.

I sat in the casting waiting room, awkwardly clutching my pepper mill, my hands slippery from sweat. It was one of those fancy pepper mills made of clear Lucite so you could see the pink and black peppercorns inside. It was over three feet tall. But it wasn't what was in my hands that made me sweat; it was the fifty or so other women my age, all of them way prettier than I was, and the lights felt more like a bright spotlight than the cool florescent bulbs they actually were. I was in the final round of casting for *The Dating Game* (embarrassing evidence that still exists in the form of old reruns on cable), and the producer had told me to bring in an object that represented me. So there I was with my pepper mill, a striking symbol of my love of cooking.

I was twenty-four, newly out of graduate school, and I had recently purchased my first home in Adams Morgan, a then-gritty but now-trendy neighborhood in Washington, DC. To celebrate my first real-estate purchase, I had bought that ridiculously oversized pepper mill at Williams-Sonoma. I almost didn't buy it. Its price didn't make sense for my salary and my student loans, but cooking was where I felt the most authentic, and I remembered Mom always telling me not to hesitate to invest in myself. So I bought the pepper mill and used it every time I gathered throngs of friends who would amicably squish into my small studio apartment, making enough noise to annoy my neighbors who had more reasonably sized dinner parties. This pepper mill was an outward representation of what I was most proud of in my twenties: after working hard and earning an MBA, I had a great job as a consultant for a large, well-known firm, and, having saved smartly, I had bought my own condo where I could finally entertain. Cooking for friends filled me up and made me feel connected.

The pepper mill worked: I booked the spot on *The Dating Game,* and on the show I selected a sweet guy named Dan (or was it Dave?). We won a getaway vacation to a top culinary program—the perfect prize for the Pepper Mill Girl and her guy, though I ended up declining. Vacationing with a stranger felt super weird. Besides, I wasn't in it for the date. It was the show itself that interested me.

This was during a big chunk of my life after my mom died when I hungered for a career in the spotlight. I'd grown up a performer, taking years of theater classes, performing in high school musicals and entertaining on cruise ships. My senior year of high school, I was cast in a pre-Broadway run of a dramatic musical called *Marmara the Gypsy* at the Kennedy Center in DC. The *Washington Post* review was scathing, leading with a headline predicting "No Tomorrow for Marmara." Five days later, the show closed abruptly, and needless to say, we never made it to Broadway. No tomorrow, indeed. The show was admittedly awful, but that tiny promise of Broadway sparked a dream. During this phase, I treated my MBA career like a backup plan—a day job that paid better than waitressing.

I studied method acting, commercial acting, and film acting. What I loved most, though, was comedy and improvisation, which I studied under Paul Sills (who founded Chicago's Second City), and I spent several seasons studying at the Groundlings. I was even inducted into the Friars Club of Beverly Hills as its youngest female member. I wasn't awful, but I wasn't great either. Still, I got to do cool things like attend famous roasts and hang out with brilliant comics and writers at the bar. Once, I chatted with Cyd Charisse in the ladies' room at Milton Berle's ninetieth birthday party. I loved getting to meet some of the greats even though I wasn't nearly talented enough to become one of them.

Later, when I was a finance manager at Disney, *The View* was created, and I even pitched myself to my colleagues at ABC as a wild-card business-voice blonde. (I did not get an audition.) One night at a dinner in Paris with my boss, Tom Staggs, who was CFO of Disney, and Anne Sweeney, who was head of ABC, I pitched the idea of a talk show where all the guests were business celebrities instead of actors and models. Once I sold them on the idea, I planned to move to my next idea: I would host and ask all those wildly insightful questions about finance, strategy, and business success, like a podcast before its time. Tom and Anne hated my show pitch, so I never even got to the part about becoming the host.

I did enough commercial work to pay my rent (barely), but luckily

I had an MBA and a "real job" to subsidize the improv, acting classes, and headshots. Then one day I got a phone call about my big break: a small role on the daytime dramatic series *General Hospital*. I played an obnoxious, high-powered businesswoman who wore a cream-colored silk blouse with an oversized gold chain design on it. I thought this could easily turn into a recurring role.

It did not.

I even hosted my first food show, *The Gourmet Gallery,* which aired only in Southern California. I cohosted with a fresh-faced red-head named Scoot. We interviewed chefs in Los Angeles and show-cased their food. Best of all, we got to eat for free at the end of each episode. But Scoot and Melissa never became Regis and Kathie Lee.

Still, I felt sure I was headed for eventual success after all my hustle. Not a day went by when I didn't call, mail, network, or claw my way into an audition, showcase, or open mic. I studied my craft, had a great agent, stayed in shape, and delivered headshots and reels around town. I listened to tapes and seminars about how to achieve your dreams and attended a Tony Robbins conference back when his hot-coal-walking exercise was new and controversial. I was crushed when audition callbacks became calls from my agent that "they went another direction." *The Dating Game* was just another appearance that came and went without any fanfare or big breaks. My dreams did not come true. Not the way I wanted them to anyway. I kept wondering why I would have a dream so clearly etched in my heart but not have the ability to bring it to fruition. I was so sure that my dreams were God's dreams too.

Trusting God is easy when the results don't really matter. Like when we are praying for a parking spot. But do we trust him when the results really matter to us? Do we dare trust him with our dreams? Do we dare suit up and show up for our day, put in the work, and let God decide the results? Especially when life is disappointing—for example, when we lose our job or are unable to realize a dream—it's easy to feel like he's forgotten us. But what if we shifted our thinking? Perhaps God is doing us a favor: removing a detour or distraction from whatever is his best for us. Like the time God didn't let me become a television star, and it led to something better.

Trusting Our Identity to God

I don't regret a minute of giving my artistic energy to a world that would seemingly not have me. My job in life is to show up and do my part. Not only am I fine with the less-than-hoped-for results I experienced, but I'm tremendously grateful that God didn't give me overwhelming success in any of those ventures. *Sometimes God does for us what we cannot do (or are not brave enough to do) for ourselves.* Of course, this acceptance is speaking from age, experience, wisdom, and hindsight. But it's also knowing that, so far, God has not dropped me even when I dropped him.

I was in the middle of my decade of grief over losing my mom and any sense of belonging. I was so completely untethered that any success in fickle show business would probably (certainly?) have ruined me. God wasn't keeping me from my dreams out of stinginess; I believe now he was protecting me from full ruin. And if I'm brutally honest, I can't even say that my motives behind the art were pure: I went onstage to escape the hard work of loving myself behind the scenes. I was chasing others' approval that I hoped might allow me to exhale and feel okay. I was seeking a sense of identity that God was aching to give me. That pepper mill could have been an emblem of servant hospitality, but my intentions were far less pure: I was hoping for stardom and adoration.

What God wanted for me all along was for me to be me. And to do it for his glory, not for mine. In escaping myself, I wasn't leaning into the me God had created. And I certainly wasn't doing any of it for his glory. You may be wondering about yourself: *Is just being me enough for God?* Yes. Yes, it is. We are enough today, with our flaws, with our baggage, with our messes, and with the bodies, houses, bank accounts, careers, and lives we have today, right this second. We are enough right now. Does that sound impossible? Read Psalm 19, where the skies actually praise God without so much as a voice. Their worship is simply in *being:* "The heavens declare the glory of God; the skies proclaim the work of his hands. . . . They have no speech, they use no words; no sound is heard from them. Yet their voice goes out into all the earth, their words to the ends of the world" (verses 1, 3–4). Just as God is praised by a sky being a sky or a tree being a tree, *being our truest self* is a form of worship.

We don't need to be successful on television and be adored by fans to find our worth. And the extra good news is that God loves you and me no matter how far off track we go. The best way we could thank him is by finding our way back to his best vision for us; the self God created us to be. We were purposefully made for something, and embracing that instead of whatever magazines and the world say we should be is showing up for our authentic, true selves.

Trusting God with our dreams takes faith. I've heard faith compared to stepping onto a bridge: you can see the bridge and believe it's there, but you don't really know its strength until you step out in faith, stand on the bridge, and put your full weight onto it. Losing at my life's dream put my entire body right there on that bridge of faith in God.

And that was right when I received an offer to move to Paris with Disney. I turned down the offer twice. When Disney came back a third time with an even better offer, I paused and prayed: *Is this the path you want for me, Lord, even if it means leaving my agent and the auditions?* Somehow deep in my soul, I felt peace that God had plans for me in France even if I didn't understand them. I broke up with Hollywood and moved to Paris. I didn't give up my dreams when I gave them up to God. I trusted them to his care, to shape and morph as he saw fit, and kept showing up each day in prayer and with my to-do list to the life he was laying out before me. God led me away from the world of auditions, to a life in Paris, and eventually to Philippe and my four daughters. And for the first time in years—moving to France, with my cat, Susie, sitting underneath the seat in front of me on that Air France flight—my soul felt calm, thanks to the wisdom of God's direction.

Following Directions

A decade later, I found out why God had put those dreams so clearly into my heart. And once again, he used food to help me on my path. With zero hustle, with no professional headshots, and with the body of a woman who had recently birthed four children, I found myself on national television. I'm not suggesting that hard work isn't required in life. But I do wonder if we can sometimes push against doors over and over when instead we need to listen for God's quiet whisper of redirection. *Not this door,* he tells us. Or *Not now.*

If you feel like you might be spending your life riding on a horse that is going in a different direction, it might be worth considering turning around on the saddle and facing the same direction as the horse. Maybe the horse is leading you to great things. Maybe instead of holding a posture of fighting for and taking control of your success, you can consider adopting a posture of receiving that reminds you of your dependence on God and keeps you grateful.

This second time I headed for television, everything was different. My focus was on how I might serve the world. How I could make the world a slightly better place for even one person by sharing my love for food and my tips for feeding a family affordably. On *The Next Food Network Star,* I was eager to share with others some of the experiences I'd had in the trenches of parenting and cooking on a budget. When I made an audition video about yogurt, my focus was on helping other moms learn what I'd learned, and I wanted them to avoid the pitfalls they might face. It was the first time I had been in front of a camera when I wasn't obsessed with how I looked or how I sounded (because, *blech,* I've always hated my voice on tape!). Good thing. I was forty years old, long past the ideal age to start a television career, was covered in baby weight, and was growing out a horrible haircut that happened in a misguided pregnancy hormone-fueled moment of "wanting a change." How wonderful that God saved my television career for a time when I could not possibly get confused and think it was because I was actually amazing or gorgeous or Hollywood-worthy!

Perhaps God waited to give me any measure of success on television until he knew he could trust me with everything that comes with being on television. I adore television and particularly love a rich, deep, authentic story, but big platforms are a slippery place to live, especially for the youthful or untethered. I had been both in my twenties.

I'm grateful God saved my television career for later in life. The strange truth about being the star of a TV show is that people treat you differently, and it's easy to get confused about who you are and where your value comes from. For instance, I was filming *Ten Dollar Dinners* and had a production assistant assigned just to me. Basically, this person's sole job was to get me whatever I needed. If I yawned on set, within minutes I'd have my exact cappuccino order in my hands from my favorite coffee place. On my lunch break, my favorite grilled salmon salad was already set up in my dressing room, along with a selection of treats from a cupcake store I'd happened to mention one day and, of course, another coffee—this time an espresso with a splash of cream, my after-lunch go-to. If I crossed my arms on set because I was cold, the air-conditioning would be cut, and one time I mentioned to a cameraman about walking around barefoot on hotel carpet, and a new pair of slippers magically appeared in my suite that evening. Cool, right? You can see how quickly this kind of treatment can turn wants into needs and foster a sense of entitlement. How easy it is to believe that I wield this kind of power because I deserve it somehow more than the forty other people working just as hard as I was on set. And this is just the privilege afforded as the host of *Ten Dollar Dinners*. Imagine if I were really famous!

God showed me an important truth about celebrity, value, and identity, again at a table. This time, it was the caterer's table at one of my early commercial shoots after winning *The Next Food Network Star*. We were filming out in the middle of nowhere, and we broke for lunch. Since there were no nearby restaurants to deliver salmon salad, I would eat my food from the on-set catering (which is, by the way, usually amazing). The director told me to change out of my wardrobe and then to head to the front of the lunch line and grab my meal. By the time I left my trailer in my own outfit, the line for food was long, filled with cameramen, producers, and crew I didn't even know existed. (It takes a lot of people to make television!) I was supposed to waltz in front of everyone to get my food first? That seemed rude! Who was I to step in front of everyone? No, I wouldn't become one of those celebrities who thought they were too good to wait in the hot sun for their meal like everyone else was. Standing in the back of the line, basking in my own congratulations for being so humble and awesome, I felt a tap on my shoulder. It was the director. He wasn't happy: "What are you doing at the back of the line?" I aw-shucks'ed my way through an explanation about being willing to wait my turn, but he cut me off. "We need you to eat first because we need you back for hair and makeup in order for us stay on schedule. Otherwise all these people have to wait for you, and it's a waste of our time." Gulp.

I never forgot that. I wasn't cutting the line because I was *worth more* than anyone else. I was just a potential bottleneck. I realized then that the star of any show is essentially what they call in show business a "continuity risk." When a scene is shot more than once and then edited together, continuity in filming means that the editor needs to make sure the second shot looks like the first shot. Sometimes, after editing, you can notice slight differences in the takes, like if the hair is brushed back in one take but forward in another. That is a continuity problem. If I am the only one in front of the camera, I am suddenly a huge continuity risk. If a cameraman comes down with the flu, they can replace him halfway through the shoot. But it's impossible to keep shooting with a different person in front of the camera. So if I'm tired and make a mistake that requires us to cut and start over, we can lose a half hour with clearing the food, resetting, and touching up hair, makeup, and wardrobe. A half hour of studio and crew time is expensive! That assistant who was paid to have a cappuccino on standby is relatively cheap insurance against losing that half hour. The way I was treated had nothing to do with my value as a human being. But I can see how celebrities can start to think that it does. When having people jump at our every whim becomes our new normal, we can start to expect the same from everyone. There is no question that would have happened to me had I gotten what I had prayed for in my twenties. What amazing grace God had *not* to give me what I begged for! He could have turned that *General Hospital* role into a full career if he had wanted, but I am convinced that my ending would not have been a happy one.

I would have been intolerable as the twenty-five-year-old television star I wanted to be, but more importantly, I would have missed out on a life doing what I believe God wants me to do with the gifts he has given me. I would have missed out on being the me I get to be today, the one I believe is more in line with God's vision for the real, unadorned me. Simply being who we are is praise to God. I know in my soul that I am meant to cook and connect with people. The exact mechanism for sharing my gifts is really none of my business. I show up and do the work I believe God has called me to do to make my own mark on the world, but it's out of obedience to God, not the need for approval or identity.

I'll say something else that may surprise you. If you feel as though God is calling you to do something, you don't have to be good at it before you obey. No one is ever good at the beginning. And even seasoned pros sometimes feel inadequate. Sitting down to write, for example, I often see the blank page and worry that what I have to write won't be good. Guess what? It won't be. Drafts rarely are. But God doesn't ask me to be good; he asks me to be obedient. I do believe that God doesn't call the equipped; he equips the called. So I show up and do the authentic work in obedience to God and let him handle what happens next.

Food and Authenticity

In Ephesians, Paul describes biblical authenticity as "put[ting] off your old self" in order "to be made new in the attitude of your minds; and to put on the new self, created to be like God in true righteousness and holiness" (4:22–24). God used a career in food to take me from my old self and bring me back to his vision for me, but the wonderful truth is that food invites us all into authenticity. We were given food from the moment we were created, and our job is to show up, tend to the garden, and receive the gift in gratitude. Like Adam and Eve, we let our sinful nature complicate things, and we want to hide behind fig leaves and wear whatever masks society tells us we need to don to be beautiful. We are left with hearts that cry out for authenticity and for God's truth, and current food culture can feel like a mockery of the simple beauty of food. Every bite we take can bring us closer to God as we practice receiving instead of taking. Perhaps we are our true selves around a dining room table more than any other spot in the home. Food reminds us all that we have nothing to hide from our Maker. How wonderful that God chose to place food into my life's dreams and purpose, but his invitation would have been as compelling, his grace just as transformative, had it been just me in a kitchen, cooking for my family on a Tuesday night.

Creating recipes and simple home cooking have become for me a kind of worship because *me being me* is my worship to God. I understand that someone may download my kale chip recipe only because it came up on a quick Google search. But my faithful worship, as far as I can tell, is praying over whatever I can create and then throwing my little pebble into the big lake of life. God will use those ever-widening circles however he sees fit. What a difference from how I approached my dreams in my youth.

It's good news that God doesn't value our personal preferences or dreams or comfort above his glory. He doesn't promise us a comfortable, easy life where our hard work is rewarded the way we want. Instead, God invites us to enter into the freedom that comes with being who we are, then leaving the results of our work up to him. And here is the exciting part: if we all show up to our lives, skills, and talents with the intention of sharing God's creation, then I believe God's universal invitation into authenticity, which leads us to tasting his grace, will somehow touch even the least spiritually inclined. What if we all tried to make someone we've never met feel loved and connected, in any small way, simply by making the world a better place by sharing our talents and gifts and by being who we really are? I firmly believe there is a chance they might see a tiny bit of God in that connection. Television was never that invitation for me—food was.

RSVP to the Invitation into Authenticity

- List some things you have found easy to trust God with. Then list the ways God worked to affirm that he orchestrated things for you. Next, think about something you are clutching, keeping control of in your grip and away from God. Could God be guiding you to a different path than you are imagining? Could that path lead to the version of you that is more in his image? Consider asking God to help you leave the results to him.

- Proverbs 16:3 says, "Commit to the LORD whatever you do, and he will establish your plans." Make a to-do list (or use one you already have) and make a second column. Call it "Results" or "Plans." Leave it blank and let God fill in the results or the plans for each item on your list.
- Is there something you feel called but unequipped to do? Decide right now that you are okay with being a beginner. Determine what the first step would look like. Then be obedient by showing up for the work—and let God decide what fruit will come of it.
- Food is a gift from God, and every meal is a chance to reconnect with God, one another, and our authentic selves. Think about how we can receive food in gratitude instead of taking it from the planet as if we are entitled to it. Simply expressing gratitude for each meal and each bite of food can remind us of who we are in God's eyes. Try eating a meal very slowly, praying before each bite.

Chapter 5

Rescuing a Good Recipe Gone Bad

An Invitation into Grace

Like many gifts, food and drink
can be used in wrong ways.

Food is pure and glorious, and it can connect us to our Creator. But we're human and flawed, and we can mess up and use God's gift all wrong. We can turn food into an idol and seek comfort that only God is meant to provide. The result can be mindless eating, gluttony, or entitled participation in a violent food system. Anytime we praise the creation more than its Creator, we are worshipping the wrong thing, even if that thing is good. And it's not just food that can trip us up. We can easily make idols out of our families, our volunteer work, our kids' activities, our churches. Gifts like food and wine, which make us feel good, can easily slide us down a slippery slope into darker elements of pleasure, such as greed and gluttony.

Like any of God's gifts, food and drink can be misused. On a rough day our sinful nature tells us that we can take the edge off by scarfing down a few cupcakes or an entire pizza without giving a passing thought to the small miracle that we can have tomato sauce and cheese and pepperoni delivered to our doorstep in thirty minutes. Or we find ourselves bored at our kids' soccer games, so we bring vats of margaritas—just enough to make the third graders' game tolerable, if not actually interesting—and share with other parents also itching to numb themselves. And while we are on this topic . . . Then we post on social media cute memes to validate the dangerous "mommy juice" narrative that parenting is so hard we need the help of alcohol just to get through it. The posts may seem harmless and funny, but at their core they glorify the abuse of God's gifts. I am not trying to demonize social drinking, but the casualness of this current must-drink-to-parent or day-drinking-is-totally-okay messaging is troubling at best and probably incredibly triggering for the sizable population who should be abstaining completely. Even those who can eat and drink normally misuse God's gift if their intention is to blot out life.

Remember that God created a food system that tells us with each bite how dependent we are on him. When we separate ourselves from the origins of our food, our ignorance invites abusing the holy aspect of God's gifts. So much of this ignorance is chosen; we place convenience, budget, and saving time higher on the totem pole, and we quietly push honoring God further down. We don't have to become farmers to honor God's food system, but most of us could stand to learn a bit more about the source of what we eat and drink. Most of us can name the last delicious dish we ate, and we can describe in detail what it tasted like, and we can recall its aroma and how it delighted our senses as we ate it. But like most modern eaters, few of us probably paused to consider where the ingredients came from before they arrived at the super-market. We know painfully little about whether we are participating in a helpful or harmful food practice.

Food is a tempting and delicious place for us to give undue power, which is part of why so many of us struggle in our relationships with it. It's not a coincidence that food was central to the humans' first act of obedience and their first act of disobedience. Satan sweet-talked Adam and Eve into eating from the one forbidden tree in the Garden of Eden, and later Satan even tried to tempt Jesus to turn stones into food when he hadn't eaten in forty days. (Unlike Adam and Eve, Jesus resisted.) When we turn to food to fill our souls and soothe them, we are replacing God with it.

Anything we make more important than God will become prob-lematic: food, alcohol, money, success, or even our children or spouses. It's tempting to replace God with things that we can touch and feel and show off to our friends. But more subtle foes also exist. Worshipping our role as awesome parents who post our children's every award on Facebook is one example. Or, as I noticed while writing this book, I started replacing my devotional and prayer time with writing. Creating a life *about* God instead of *with* him can separate us from him because our sinful nature is clever and tricky. But the good news is, God's grace is truly sufficient for us all.

An Uncomfortable Lesson in Grace

Just after college, I was working on a ship that sailed around Greece, Turkey, Israel, and Egypt, and occasionally I acted as a guide on the ship's shore excursions. After one particular salty beach trip to the Dead Sea, we headed to lunch. Gorgeous platters of food were placed in front of us, and God's glory was on full display. Thinly sliced dried meats and charcuterie, plump and brightly colored roasted vegetables marinated in a bright citrus oil, and jagged cubes of dried, pressed cheese curds drizzled with a fragrant olive oil thick with herbs all begged to be scooped up with hunks of bread, still warm and yeasty. Pitchers of chilled pink wine were served, less sweet than I had feared, the grapes rich from their days in the sun.

I sat among this crowd of cruise-ship passengers from all over the world, near-strangers, sharing our experiences. During that week we'd seen the Wailing Wall and Paul's prison and the Jordan River, and we'd communicated in a mishmash of several languages. I settled into the feeling of being fed by the food and the relaxing warmth of the wine when someone toasted Jesus for wisely suggesting wine as a symbol for his blood. The passenger was half joking and we laughed, but I felt a tinge of uneasiness, not quite able to put my finger on the complicated relationship between food and drink and God. The truth was, ever since my mom died the year before, I had noticed my drinking increasing. I fell within the parameters of what might be considered normal for a twenty-one-year-old, but inside me something awoke in this moment. It was the first time I had ever considered that how I drank might not be what God wanted for me. I knew a fair amount about wine, and I respect that a good glass of wine represents a lot of careful cultivation and creation. But that's not all I know about wine. I've seen the glory, and I've also seen the devastation.

But I didn't see it right away. In fact, I spent years drinking on a subtle, slow slope filled with mixed results. Most of the time, I was a purely delightful social drinker, who every now and again drank enough to warrant a headache the next day. Nothing a few Tylenol and a large Coke couldn't handle. But I couldn't deny that over the years the small headaches turned into actual hangovers, and I couldn't predict which evenings would lead to a rough morning and which wouldn't. Quite simply, if I had a first drink, I couldn't be sure what the next day would be like. Most were okay, but some were not, and those not-okay mornings were happening more often. The acceleration concerned me, but then there were the many times when I'd have a drink or two and be just fine. I clung to them as evidence that nothing was wrong.

Then the Plum Tree Inn incident happened.

I attended a Christian singles mixer at a trendy Los Angeles spot called the Plum Tree Inn. I walked into this restaurant filled with strangers, and I immediately felt out of my comfort zone. I'm an introvert. Parties are awkward to navigate because I almost always would rather be home sitting on my couch, reading a book. Add to that mix a lifetime of growing up being the "smart" one while my sister was the "pretty" one. And then there's the strong family propensity to avoid conflict through medicating.

I headed straight for the bar. I don't even recall if I considered the fact that I was driving. I was so uncomfortable that if I had, it didn't matter to me in that moment. As the evening went on, we rotated seats at every course so we could meet even more people. This was meant to be fun, I'm sure, but it was not for me. With each new place setting, I started a new glass of red wine to fortify myself for the inevitable round of introductions and small talk. I don't think I ate much at that dinner, but I drank plenty.

Fortunately, the Los Angeles Police Department was on its game that night. I was pulled over moments after I backed out of my parking spot. After miserably failing dexterity tests that I fear I would fail today stone-cold sober, we had what I considered a very amicable arrest. I was a willing participant, friendly even. I applauded the LAPD for its fine work and keen eye in pulling me off the road. All this was going swimmingly, so I thought. Maybe these nice officers would drive me home. Maybe one of them would follow behind in the car I was too drunk to drive, saving me the hassle of returning the next day with a taxi. But my ridiculous read of the situation evaporated when they slapped handcuffs on my wrists. Suddenly I was sobbing and being led into the back of a cop car, my head gingerly protected by the officer's hand as I ducked into the back seat.

I spent that night in jail. I still recall the outfit I wore: a gorgeous green silk blouse under my favorite St. John suit. I was classic corporate conservative, having spent my entire career in corporate finance during a period when women were not allowed to wear pants to work, and we were "strongly discouraged" from wearing separates because a dark suit was what was required to get ahead in the male-dominated climate of success. I remember thinking how pitiful my mug shot would be: budding young corporate executive, wearing an expensive suit, tears of disbelief smearing her carefully applied mascara. Years later, I laughed at the ridiculousness of my choosing this outfit for a casual dinner for twentysomethings looking to meet a mate. I don't remember what everyone else was wearing, because it was decades ago and apparently I was quite drunk, but I imagine that in a sea of people dressed in trendy clothes from Abercrombie, I stood out as the only one dressed like Hillary Clinton. (I mean that very literally. I owned several of the exact same suits that Clinton wore in the nineties.) Talk about the wrong outfit for the occasion! But I digress.

You want to find out who your friends are? Go to jail. Turns out, the movies are right: you really do get only one phone call. In the middle of the night, I called my girlfriends Dell and Karen, who were roommates at the time. With my small weak voice, I begged them through their answering machine to pick up the phone. They did.

The next morning, Dell and Karen took me to the impound lot to pick up my car. So many cars in the LA impound lot were smashed up, clearly driven by people who were either in the hospital or in the morgue. I looked past these cars that were merely rubble from unspeakable accidents, some with rusty edges, some likely never to be claimed by their owners. And suddenly through the dusty, depressing scene, I saw my leased car way in the back—unblemished. My first real grown-up car, this shiny four-door sedan with leather seats that made me feel successful. But that day, my beautifully maintained, gold-toned car meant one thing to me: a do-over that the owners of so many cars on that lot had not been given.

I imagined for a moment that the situation had not turned out this well. *What if I had hurt myself or—worse—someone else? What if my car had been smashed up like these other cars?* I stood quietly for a few minutes, saying nothing, letting this reality sink in. There on the West LA car impound lot, I prayed as I had never prayed before. I pleaded with God, full of regret, begging for one more chance, like a kid pleading with her mom when a deeply treasured item has been taken away. I imagined, for a moment, God thinking it through and then slowly telling me: *Okay, but just one chance.* Tears dropped onto the dusty ground as I prayed my most sincere prayer since before my mom had died: "I hear you. I feel you. And I won't waste my last chance."

That is how I learned about grace. And gratitude. I've been living on my second chance ever since.

In that moment, under the warm spring sun of Los Angeles, my ten-year spiritual winter ended.

But day-to-day life had changed. Life complicated by legal woes was hard. DUI lawyers want to be paid in cash (who can blame them?), so I suddenly had no money despite having a great job. Respectable insurance companies drop you, and you're stuck paying four or five times the price for the auto insurance you see advertised on late-night television. You also lose your license for a while, which makes getting to work in Los Angeles a major hassle. I practically lived off the leftover bagels that were delivered every morning to my office's kitchen, and if I worked long enough hours (which I usually did), I made dinner out of whatever kitchen snacks were provided by my employer—pumpkin seeds, Red Vines (a sacrifice for this die-hard Twizzlers fanatic), and hard crunchy pretzels from Costco-sized bins. If I ever wanted a beer to take the edge off the crumminess of the day, now was the time. But I didn't. I suspected from my mom's suicide what kind of family genes I was up against. I got sober and have stayed sober one day at a time for more than twenty years—and counting.

My self-identity had also changed: I found God again. I had always known he was there, but my prayer at the impound lot jump-started my prayer life, and I started and ended every single day on my knees on the floor just next to my bed. My daily prayers made the logistics of my legal mess feel doable. I showed up to God and found that he had been there throughout those years while I all but ignored him. I also worked the twelve steps, which I'm still convinced was the best therapy I could have hoped to find. I leaned into my powerlessness and God's strength. I grew to believe truly that when I am weak, he is strong. I grew to be thankful—truly thankful—for everything, and my gratitude was sincere because in God's grace, I found complete love, acceptance, and peace.

Once again, I believe God did for me what I could not do for myself: he taught me that my identity and value aren't in what I do, but in who I am in him. Not my career, not my smarts, not my clothes, not my boyfriend, not the super-funny-me-after-a-few-drinks. (I was a hoot after a beer or two. Not to mention a fantastic dancer. All in my own mind, of course.)

This season reminded me again that sometimes when you feel like the world is falling apart, it's actually just coming together, and that sometimes the only way out of something is to march through it. The hull of the seed is destroyed to make way for something new to grow from that seed. Sending Jesus to us was the ultimate gift, and he loves us no matter how we act, including how we act with food or wine or anything else we choose to idolize.

We have such hope! God's grace is bigger than any mess we bring on ourselves, and those messes can be dark. If you've ever worried that God might give up because you've just done too much to disappoint him, I hope you hear this: Our salvation is won-and-done by Jesus, and how we act isn't how we earn his grace. How we live is our response to his grace, our thank-you letter to God. When we fully understand the magnitude of God's grace, then gratitude and obedience just make sense. That was the gift of the impound lot for me: I felt the magnitude of God's grace. And it is so huge and powerful that, even decades later, I still feel it in my bones every single minute. It is the greatest miracle of my days on earth. Perhaps I could have come to this appreciation of God's mercy without my sinful misuse of wine. But he used it all for his good as he promised he would. I don't regret my past because it's what drew me closer to God than I had ever imagined and gave me a truly glorious future. God used that awful night in jail for my good, just as he promised to do in Romans 8:28. And God's grace can do the same for you, whatever challenges you face.

We are deeply flawed beings, but God's grace is big enough to cover our imperfections. Perhaps you struggle with right-sizing food, or maybe a small part of you questions your own drinking. Or maybe you are worshipping something other than God, something like shopping or pornography or working out. God's grace is for you too. Hope and beauty exist when we receive God's complete and total grace. I know God's grace as surely as I know my dog is sitting at my feet as I type this. I'm in your corner, and so is God.

RSVP to the Invitation into Grace

- Make a list of some of God's biggest gifts in your life. Sit in prayer with the list and ask God to reveal anywhere you are placing the gift above the Giver.
- Learn more about the food that God gives us. Consider tracking down the sources of just a few of the products you buy the most. Some ways include researching on the internet your favorite companies, calling a company on its public information line, and heading to your local farmers market to talk to the farmers themselves. Pray for God to show you more about the food you are eating and to guide you toward food that is thoughtfully and kindly created.
- Create a gratitude list that includes both big stuff and small stuff. Gratitude is a habit, and writing even a short list daily is life changing. You will become more grateful. You will also begin to see beyond the awesomeness of the gift, and you'll better appreciate in your bones the extraordinarily generous nature of

the Giver. This perspective will help make his grace more apparent to you.

- Romans 8:28 says, "We know that in all things God works for the good of those who love him, who have been called according to his purpose." Make a list of specific examples of times when God has used your mistakes to create something for his good. What hope does this give you for your future?

Chapter 6

Rethinking Quick-Tip Recipe Shortcuts

An Invitation into Patience

Food can, and should, slow us down.

God is the original architect of the slow-food movement, which celebrates real, whole food—the opposite of fast food. He deliberately created a slow nourishment process. Our food system gives us the chance to develop patience. If you are a go-getter-high-energy person like I am, you might be thinking: *What good is that? Isn't faster better?*

We hate waiting, right? We sit in a waiting room at the doctor's office, and thank goodness there are thousands of magazines to entertain our every second. Certainly I'm not going to just sit there like a schmuck! If I choose the slow checkout line at the grocery store, I can feel my insides actually churning with annoyance. And heaven help anyone who writes an actual check, ever, because the entire store, including me, will glare at that person who made us *wait*.

Waiting makes us feel helpless, but . . . that can be a good thing. Waiting can force us to acknowledge our dependence on God. *Patience is celebrating that waiting space rather than despising it.* We might all agree that time, being irreplaceable, is our most precious resource. So when we offer it back to God by choosing patience, it's an act of trust and dependence on him. Patience also creates space for connection and growth to happen, for wisdom to form, and for character to develop. And God can use food to help bring about all of that.

Discovering True Nourishment

Patience isn't my strong suit. I've always been what you might call a type A personality. Left to my natural inclinations, I'm all go-go-go with no margin. And as a working mom of four on-the-go girls, I've learned to calculate exactly how long any given car trip will take, then work right up to the exact minute we have to hop in the minivan. In fact, as I write this, I've allocated exactly six minutes more for writing before I have to shower and head out the door for a conference. Yes, I'm that scheduled. Oh, I've heard the arguments for creating margin, but obliterating my margin and scheduling one final thing is my default mode. The irony is, however, my to-do list doesn't always reflect what I value long term. Instead, it's filled with the stuff that gives me immediate satisfaction.

If I find an unexpected fifteen minutes, I tend to hop on my computer and get a jump-start on a project or reply to a work email or scroll through social media. I don't use those unexpected minutes to pursue activities more linked to my long-term goals, like spending more time with my family or exercising. An unofficial poll of my type A friends confirms I'm not alone: we seek feedback and reward in so many of our activities that it starts to feel like any time we aren't actively in a feedback loop is a waste of time. So when the world told me in my twenties that time spent making daily meals is wasted time, I was primed and receptive to that message. Sure, I cooked to host dinner parties and dazzle my friends. But my daily meals? I ate most of them out, and if I cooked during the workweek, faster always meant better. I almost never stopped working for lunch, stuffing a forkful of salad in my mouth while typing. I definitely didn't consider the ingredient sources of any of my meals. I was far too busy even to cook, let alone to step out of my willful ignorance of whether my food choices were honoring God or breaking his heart.

When I moved to Paris in 2000, I wasn't just transformed by the ingredients there; I was changed by how Parisians ate too. Yes, Paris is a big city, and the pace is big-city fast. I was surrounded by hard workers, high achievers, and big dreamers much like me. Paris's pulsating rhythm of life matched the frantic pace of life I'd grown to love, if only out of familiarity. The City of Light seemed also never to sleep. But I soon discovered that meals in France are quite different from meals in America. French food demands time and attention, even in busy Paris.

Lesson number one came during my first week at Euro Disney, and the finance department was under a tight deadline. So when lunchtime rolled around, I expected that someone might have lunch brought in so we could continue working. Simple sandwiches would enable us to stay huddled over the work. Instead, we all closed up our desks and headed out for lunch. To this day I remember that I ordered steamed salmon and vegetables, a luxurious midday meal that might happen at my office back in Burbank only on unusually slow days like the Tuesday before Thanksgiving. And the kicker was we stopped afterward for coffee. There we were, under a huge deadline, laughing and talking

while casually sipping our espressos and nibbling on squares of chocolate served with the coffee (oh, the wisdom of the French!) as if we had
not a care in the world.

I was so puzzled during that first lunch that I thought perhaps I
had misunderstood the urgency of our deadline. I knew my French
was weak, but was I completely clueless? Clearly we wouldn't be in-
dulging in so much time away from the office when our CFO was
awaiting deliverables, right? But once we were back in the office, the
countdown was still clearly underway, and we all buried our noses in
our work. And here's the thing: I worked differently—I worked
better—after breaking for lunch. Trying to eat a sandwich without
getting crumbs in my keyboard would not have had the same effect at
all. We were refreshed by our break. We had rested our minds and
nourished both our bodies and our souls. I didn't realize it at the time,
but I was leaning into God and his rest, which invigorated me for the
work that lay ahead.

So, yes, I experienced the slow-food tradition of Paris culture, but it
hung by a thread, threatened to be overwhelmed by the hurry of global
urban life. When I first moved there, I told my colleagues all about
Starbucks, which was just taking off in a big way back in the US, excitedly suggesting that we should get one at Disney Village. I was shot
down hard. My French colleagues all agreed that French culture would
never support the idea of coffee to go; French people want to stop, enjoy
their coffee in a ceramic mug—never a paper cup—and talk to people,
not slurp an espresso down while walking down the street. Nearly two
decades later, though, that mentality has changed. Starbucks dot the
streets of Paris, each one filled with French folks who don't seem to
mind skipping the rest-and-connection part of their coffee. I do love a

good cup of Starbucks coffee, but I clearly see the wisdom of those French colleagues two decades ago.

Letting Food Slow Us Down

A few months after moving to Paris, I met Philippe, who is from a tiny village outside of Aix-en-Provence in the South of France.

Meals in the South of France have a completely different rhythm than Parisian meals. They are a whole step-function slower, and the pace shocked my type A, post-MBA, career-girl sensibilities. More time, money, and energy are put into everyday meals in France than we Americans might allocate even to special meals. The menus are deliberate, and the ingredients are procured at specialty markets—the butcher for meat, the farmers market or vegetable market for produce, and the bakery for bread. The supermarket is plan B, used in a pinch rather than the primary supplier of food. The amount of money spent on ingredients is also higher. The French seem far more comfortable spending money on quality ingredients than Americans do. No surprise there, since according to the USDA, the American food budget as a percentage of income is the lowest in the world. Part of that can be explained by relatively high American income, but a part of that is also explained by a food system that prioritizes low cost over everything else, including the long-term health of our people and land. The result is that Americans seek out uber-cheap ingredients, such as subsidized corn syrup and meat produced in conditions that make many of our European neighbors gasp. If we were to pay the true cost of food, including the external and the invisible costs, it would be much pricier, and I believe we would take greater care in its preparation and consumption.

But back to Aix-en-Provence. Lunch and dinner in the South of France can easily last a couple of hours, each mealtime filled with conversation, connections, and sometimes boisterous debate. Food brings people together, not just around the table but around the entire food life cycle. In my experience, no one knows this more innately than the French.

Philippe's mother—my mother-in-law—is one of the best home cooks I have ever known. Muriel takes the time to make everything as homemade as possible. The first time I visited her home, she apologized for the store-bought mayonnaise on the tuna baguette sandwiches she made for our beach picnic. She lets the food—both its preparation and its consumption—slow her down, and she has passed some of these lessons on to me.

Ratatouille, a classic vegetable dish starring eggplant, zucchini, peppers, onions, and tomatoes, is deeply engrained in the culture of Mediterranean France. When I married a man from the heart of Provence, one of the first lessons I received from my new mother-in-law was how to make a proper ratatouille. Turns out, my American approach had me cooking a ratatouille far too long, making it a gloppy stew of indistinguishable mixed vegetables, a crime I've seen committed more often than not here in the United States.

Muriel was kind in her rebuke and showed me her way instead. The preparation would take longer than the American way, she warned me, but it would be worth it. I was a skeptical-but-willing audience. The most important lesson was to cook each vegetable separately, to honor its individuality. Moreover, the vegetables needed to be cooked in the same pan, in a specific order, so the flavors would be built just right. (In case you are wondering, the order is eggplant, zucchini, peppers, onions, and tomatoes. I use the acronym EZ-POT to remember.) As she explained the process, my skepticism returned, and I planned to chuck this tradition out the window as soon as I got back to my own kitchen. But Muriel's version is easily the best ratatouille I have ever eaten, so I follow her recipe now without fail, even if the rebellious part of me wonders, *If I dared to cook the zucchini out of order, would anyone really notice?* But why mess with genius?

Muriel even managed to mentor me in the kitchen when I prepared my home country's national culinary treasure: Thanksgiving dinner. As the sole American in a French family, I knew early on that all the Thanksgiving cooking duties would fall squarely on me. I was happy to take on that responsibility. So, on my first Thanksgiving in France, Philippe and I took the high-speed train down from Paris to visit his family, where I planned to introduce the d'Arabian clan to the wonders of an American Thanksgiving. The only problem: turkeys in France are bred for eating at Christmas, making a November turkey impossible to find at the butcher shop.

My (then-future) father-in-law, Georges, finally tracked down a turkey we could buy for our meal through some special arrangement he made with a local farmer. When Georges greeted us at the train station after our three-hour trip from Paris, he told me we'd be picking up the turkey on the way home.

A little background here: I've been to a million farmers markets, and Paris is loaded with butcher shops displaying meat about eight steps less processed than what we are accustomed to in the United States. I mean, I saw pigs with squiggly tails and hanging rabbits still looking like Thumper. So I am not squeamish.

But when Georges pulled the car up to what looked like a private home with a large chicken coop along the side, I got nervous. Was there a storefront I had missed? Or even a processing plant nearby? There was not.

The farmer asked me to pick a turkey from the flock running around outside. I had to pick from among these cute feathery birds clucking and gobbling around me, cocking their heads to the side, hoping I had food to share. The humanity of this *Sophie's Choice* moment sank into my gut. I was forced to stop and humbly reckon with the fact that I was choosing which creature would give its life for our meal. I wanted to be worthy of receiving its gift; I wanted to honor the to-be-sacrificed bird's role in our Thanksgiving. I owed these turkeys a little bit of my time. I finally managed to choose. I also learned that day that nothing says "Welcome to the family" like plucking turkey feathers together. (If Muriel is reading this, she is surely thinking I'm being very generous to include my attempts to pluck as a meaningful part of the process. Truth be told, Muriel did most of the plucking—and all of the foot removal.) And I gained a new respect for the animals that give their lives to those who eat them.

Our dinner preparations continued. The turkey was finally looking like an ingredient and not a dinner guest, the side dishes were prepped, and I turned my attention to making my sour cream apple pie and, of course, pumpkin pie. I pulled out my refrigerated piecrust with the confidence of an accomplished cook who is simply smart about where she will spend her time. Muriel looked at me in confusion. Why would I possibly spend all day making an amazing homemade meal (did I mention I plucked, sort of?) yet use premade crust? Homemade crust is so easy and so much better, she insisted. I wasn't convinced, but in all fairness, I acknowledged that my only experience with homemade crust was with my mom's Crisco concoction (so hip in the seventies!), that tasted like, well, vegetable oil. And since my mom wasn't alive to defend herself, I suppose I never felt right pointing out how dreadful her piecrust always was. And let me say: refrigerated piecrust can be a life-saver on a crazy busy day, so know that I'm not against the occasional convenience food. But living and cooking and eating in France had me rethinking convenience food being plan A. That Thanksgiving Day we used refrigerated piecrust, and my dinner landed on the table on schedule. But the turkey already had me rethinking our food system and my role in slowing down a little for it.

Still, it wasn't until the week before my wedding that I learned how to make Muriel's piecrust. Why several years after that first Thanksgiving incident? I don't know. Maybe Muriel sensed it was a tender topic, replacing my mom's awful crust with a fabulous one? Or perhaps that was my doing. Sometimes you can put out a vibe without meaning to. I think that in a small way, with the wedding around the corner, Muriel wanted to let me know that while she'll never be able to replace my mom, she would be like a mom to me. She wanted us to share more than just the moniker "Madame d'Arabian." Or maybe Muriel was just tired of mediocre piecrust.

So the week before the wedding, Muriel took my hand, walked me into her kitchen, and announced to me that the "big day" was here. I thought she was reaching out for a prewedding moment, but it turns out the "big day" she was referencing was the day I would finally learn her family-famous butter piecrust recipe.

Muriel taught me how to make her simple but deliciously flaky crust using nothing but cold cubes of butter, flour, ice water, her hands, and a floured surface. She took the time to sprinkle the flour and care-fully roll out the dough, letting it rest in the pie plate before baking so it would stay tender. She was right; the time invested in making the dough yielded a flaky, buttery payoff that no premade crust could ever touch. Over the years, I adapted the recipe just slightly to make it with a food processor. Muriel insists that the food processor runs the risk of overmixing. I think, however, that pulsing the ingredients with a food processor actually means the dough is handled less and more quickly, and the butter isn't as subject to my hands' warmth. So we each have our own way of making the crust, but we both treasure those few minutes of slowing down and feeling the dough. I wish my mom could be here to learn Muriel's recipe. She would certainly scoff at the ridiculousness of her shortening version.

Ever since Muriel talked me into making butter crusts, I've never looked back. Her butter crust became the star ingredient in my fan-favorite potato-bacon torte recipe. I am often asked what my favorite dish is to cook, and this is it.

The potato-bacon torte is certainly tasty comfort food—rich with cream, slightly smoky from bacon, and deliciously encrusted with the unmistakable aroma of a buttery crust that flakes when you take a bite. The entire house smells like a fluffy warm croissant when I bake it. A small sliver and a simple green salad with a tangy Dijon vinaigrette is the perfect winter supper, if you ask me. And the recipe costs pennies a serving to make, so it aligns with the frugal me.

In 2009, I made a potato-bacon torte as part of the Ultimate Dinner Party Challenge on *The Next Food Network Star* and served it to a group of incredibly esteemed chefs, including Bobby Flay, Masaharu Morimoto, Rick Bayless, and François Payard. I was one of the three finalists fighting for a spot in the finale, and my potato-bacon torte helped me secure one of those coveted spots—and eventually win the title. So in addition to being a recipe that slowed me down, you might say that I count this recipe as one of my lucky charms.

But winning *The Next Food Network Star* isn't the reason I adore the potato-bacon torte. I love the torte because it represents so many parts of my life, all in one dish, and making the butter crust slows me down enough so I can think about those times. From my own childhood, I carry on my mom's tradition of carving steam vents in the crust in the shape of my guests' initials. The very idea of baking potato and bacon in a crust came from Muriel, who served it to me the first time I visited my husband's home village in the South of France. And since I've had my own daughters, I have served the potato-bacon torte at every one of our annual mother-daughter holiday teas.

Yes, the torte is luscious, flaky, and comforting (try it!). I do believe it's a big reason why I won my own television show, and it deserved its spot in the very first season of *Ten Dollar Dinners* and in the book *Ten Dollar Dinners*. But it's the rich history behind the torte—the memories that are baked into each one—and the care that goes into it that make it my favorite recipe. It's the people I imagine each time I make it and the people I see each time I serve it. The potato-bacon torte slowed me down and created the space for my mom's traditions to meet my mother-in-law's.

Time at the Table

It's not just the celebration of ingredients or the unhurried nature of their cooking that the French are getting right; it's also how they sit around a table, how long they stay there, and how often they share their table with one another. Meals are slow, conversation is rich, and people are welcomed to the table, often without fussy advanced preparations. There's so much I love about French eating! As a former expat but also a fiercely proud American, I can't help but create in my mind the fantasy of a perfect hybrid of both cultures—a deeply complex nirvana where I would have French cheese and tangy green salad after every meal and starchy, buttery carbs likes croissants for breakfast along with a decidedly American protein-and-veggie smoothie. The truth is, taking only the best parts of two cultures is nearly impossible because those cultural gems that we see and perhaps even envy are linked inexorably to the rest of the culture's history, quirks, and characteristics. France's longer lunches and extended vacation times were divine. But they are deeply rooted in a culture that values personal time more highly than we do in the United States. I loved the idea of leisurely meals, but my corporate American training had me also quite frustrated at the slow pace of getting consensus on an important work project. I'd try to book a meeting with colleagues and find, statistically speaking, 20 percent of them away on vacation.

Still, we are wise to learn from other cultures and take in a little from what we experience while living or even visiting overseas. One of my favorite French eating traditions is the aperitif, a convivial and family-friendly version of the American cocktail hour. More than a snack and drink break, the aperitif is a short pause taken before dinner to transition from the worries of the day into the connection of dinner. Whenever we are visiting my in-laws, an hour or two before dinnertime the family gathers around some tiny nibbles and sips on anything from sparkling water to lemonade to pastis on ice with a splash of water. An aperitif brings family and friends together, luring us gently out of our day and into the evening.

If my in-laws are any measure, the aperitif is the unofficial neighborly moment in France—not quite the five-hour commitment of a French dinner but a perfect way to spend a casual hour or two with friends from across the street. And even if we aren't invited to an aperitif or hosting friends, the large tray of beverages heading out to the back patio is a trusty reminder that dinner is about an hour away.

The food served at an aperitif varies widely. It can be as small as a bowl of olives or nuts or, oddly, decidedly American Pringles. Or it can be a near-buffet of heartier finger fare, called an *aperitif dinatoire.* Some favorites of ours to serve include *pissaladière* (caramelized onion tart), tapenade, and pâté and toasted country bread. Sometimes at the *apero* (as it's often called) the chatting keeps going past dinner hour. Often the neighbors linger, and we find ourselves digging through the fridge to find something to toss on the grill or some kind of leftovers to turn into an impromptu dinner party. No stress. No Pinterest-perusing to find the just-right recipe. Just the gift of time shared with family or friends that extends into a meal because no one wants the connection to end.

French meals slowed me down. By prioritizing speed and saving money over everything else, we are missing out not just on God's will for us but also on his best for us. We miss out on the daily reminder to give God space, to offer him our time, and to develop our patience.

When the food industry gave us fast food, I don't think we understood the price we would pay for that convenience. Planning our meals, getting ingredients, cooking our food, serving it at a table where we sit and connect—these activities slow us down enough to be able to bond with one another and with God. We all need time for gratitude and connection and rest. Let's choose to be patient and wait for our produce to be in season rather than insisting on peach pies in January. Let's slow down and savor God's food. Let's take the time to find the right ingredients. To pluck the turkey. To make the dough. To let the stew simmer gently. And to sit at the table long enough to connect beyond the small talk.

Not every dinner needs to be a full-fledged production. After all, we live in a modern world with demands on our time. But perhaps we can at least value the patience that God's food system encourages.

RSVP to the Invitation into Patience

- Find a recipe that takes a while to make, and then make it. It doesn't have to be a complicated recipe but just one that takes its time to develop its flavors, like a nice braise or stew or hearty soup. Savor the smells in the kitchen, and when it's ready, eat slowly. What do you notice about the meal?
- Think of a time when God answered a prayer a long while after you prayed it. List the benefits of waiting, and the blessings of that waiting period. Could the prayer have been answered properly earlier than it was?
- James 5:7 tells us to be patient like the farmer is patient in waiting for his crops. Psalm 31:15 says to God, "My times are in your hands." Do you commit your time to God? Does this time include the time spent on procuring, preparing, and eating your food? Your to-do list? Your long-term and short-term plans? What does it not currently include?

Chapter 7

Loving Our Family's Legacy

An Invitation into Connection

Food can connect us to
one another and to God.

Sometimes I forget that I'm not flying solo. None of us is. We are part of a bigger story that includes God as well as people who went before us and who will come after us, and we get to decide how we play our part. God uses food to support that connection to one another, but also our connection to him and to creation. He wants to be in communion with us, and food is part of that vertical link. And it is part of a very intimate connection we have with every other creature and plant on this planet. Think about this: we literally take into our bodies the DNA of animals and of plants that were raised in soil made rich by the life and death of other plants, animals, and, yes, human beings. That's a deep bond we share!

We are meant to connect and are hardwired for relationship. We are pack animals! God says in Genesis 2:18 that "it is not good for the man to be alone," and we are described throughout the Bible as being parts of the same body and bricks of the same building. Food connects us not only with the people in our lives today but also with the people who went before us, who are part of our history, even if we have never met. We stand on the shoulders of our ancestors and leave a legacy for our children, and food is part of that legacy. Connecting our past with our future feels right, and it is why we universally treasure our grandmother's recipes for homemade sauces, meatballs, and cakes. Nothing connects us to our heritage like a recipe handed down through the generations.

The Power of Food Connections

So much of what I know about life I learned from my mom. She taught me to work hard, be kind, have a sense of humor, and welcome people into my home and heart. Even though Mom cooked the same five or ten dishes most of the time, she threw a big cookie party every year around Christmas. As stressed as she was about the financial and logistical aspects of feeding us daily, Mom was completely free from that bondage when she hosted. The menu was simple by most standards—cookies galore—but she seemed her happiest when guests would fill up their plates. From that, I learned to find joy in cooking for others. For years, Mom's holiday party and her food-budget savvy made up the entirety of her culinary heritage.

My mom's cooking repertoire consisted of recipes she followed faithfully. All of her personal recipes could fit in a shoebox. She kept those she liked best—her "family recipes"—in a two-toned mustard-yellow and avocado-green plastic recipe box with Betty Crocker's spoon embossed on the front lip. That box, my mother's entire cooking legacy, was lost when she died. I was twenty years old, in college, and overwhelmed. So rather than review all her things and carefully select a few meaningful mementos, I kept it all and sent everything across the country to be stored indefinitely in my grandmother's garage. I simply could not part with any of it, so I kept it all, naively imagining that someday I would have the time and energy to review everything with a more discerning eye. I stuffed Grandma's four-car garage half-full of boxes brimming with old magazines, tired silverware, and women's suits that would be out of style by the time I had a job worthy of wearing them. And someday never came . . . because someday never does.

Over the years, Mom's things were lost, donated, or ruined by water damage and time. And since I lived thousands of miles away, most of my mother's belongings became less important to me as the years ticked by. I've realized, though, that by holding on to everything, I kept track of nothing. I lost even those things that might have mattered . . . if I'd known what they were.

Still, I managed to create my own culinary identity beginning even in those empty years of isolation after Mom's suicide. Without much input from my past and without much connection to anything in the present, I started to become my own person in the kitchen. As I've already mentioned, in my twenties I hosted dinner parties, cramming fifty people into my tiny and stuffy Washington, DC, apartment. Hosting people awakened my connection to Mom, who was at her best when people were in our home. Living in Paris in my thirties taught me to cook without a recipe. When I married Philippe, my mother-in-law shared her legacy of Southern French country fare—home cooking at its best.

My grandmother on my father's side shared her German roots with me through her recipes of comforting, meaty, braised rouladen and tangy cabbage and apples. When my precious grandma died at ninety-two, I mourned the loss of what little anchor I'd had; her address was the permanent address I'd used on important forms. My husband flew out to empty her garage. There he found the green-and-yellow box with the iconic Betty Crocker spoon emblazoned on the front. Grandma had kept my mother's little box of recipes for me all those years, and in her death, she reconnected me to my past.

My mom had organized her entire life on three-by-five-inch index cards, and her recipe collection was no exception. She'd stuffed that box with cards (mostly) and scrap paper written in her distinct handwriting, forming sentences and paragraphs I had never seen. I was thrilled. I hadn't seen anything new from my mom in more than twenty years. Discovering new memories about a long-lost loved one has its own kind of special joy that feels a little like hearing that person's voice again, if only for a minute.

Philippe lovingly pulled every recipe and made copies of the decaying slips of paper, deciphered the water-smudged ink on the cards, and made me a keepsake book. Most of Mom's recipes were from friends, and she'd named them accordingly: Karen's Company Chicken, Libby's Dip. (No last names because apparently only one Karen mattered to Mom.)

The recipe box confirmed something else: my mother truly was a mediocre and limited cook. She had taken a few cooking classes later in her life once she had the money, but I saw in the three-by-five cards almost no evidence of a sophisticated palate. Given that this box represented a lifetime in the kitchen, there were woefully few recipes, and none were particularly fancy. No fewer than three (three!) were variations of a broccoli-cheese casserole. How had a woman whose best dishes starred canned cream of mushroom soup and buttered bread-crumbs taught me how to cook?

The answer is, she taught me to love, and she showed me that cooking for people was an outward expression of that love. She inspired me to cook for the people, not the plate. My mom taught me to value a big pot of chili shared with loved ones over a five-star meal eaten alone. She embodied the wisdom of Proverbs 15:17: "A bowl of vegetables with someone you love is better than steak with someone you hate" (NLT).

From that recipe box I also discovered that recipes don't have to be sophisticated, or even all that tasty, to be meaningful. Libby's Dip is a weird concoction of hard-boiled eggs, pickle relish, cheddar cheese, and chopped olives. Perhaps it wouldn't be my first choice to serve at a dinner party, but I'm transported back to my childhood just thinking about the combination melted together and then spooned onto a Wheat Thin, the official cracker of my youth. I've even learned to update Mom's recipes to suit our tastes, which is what I did with her famous flank steak recipe. Her flank steak is the family recipe that I most closely associate with my mom. Making it takes me right back to my childhood—the aroma of the sizzling steak, the tangy sauce that I would slurp up with the spoon. It was reserved for special occasions like birthdays or Christmas, and even then, my mom swapped out the olive oil for vegetable oil because olive oil was too expensive. The flank steak tradition has continued with my own family. I make it by request for several birthdays each year, and I even created a tofu version for my vegetarian daughter who grew up loving this dish. The smell and the taste of flank steak always remind me of being a kid myself, which is a rare gift for me.

Marrying Philippe brought the recipes of his relatives to add to our family's history. A favorite family recipe comes from Philippe's grand-mother, or "Mamy," who is ninety-three and lives in Nice in the South of France. She's famous for her *coca*, a typical dish from Nice. *Coca* is a savory pastry, something like a very thin pizza crust filled with an aro-matic mixture of tomatoes, peppers, onions, and herbs cooked down into a thick flavorful paste. *Coca* has been served at every single d'Arabian event I recall ever attending in the two decades I have been part of the family. Several years ago, the younger generation took over the somewhat labor-intensive task of making the *coca*, so Mamy was required to share her secret recipe. So far, though, no one has been able to replicate the exact taste of Mamy's *coca* that we know and love. At every family gathering, my husband and my brother-in-law good-naturedly tease Mamy that she is holding out on some part of the rec-ipe. She insists that she isn't. We may never know how to make Mamy's exact *coca*, but that may be part of the joy and the legacy. It's certainly part of the story we all tell when we make it.

Food traditions connect us to our past, but they also connect us to one another. Back when Mamy still made the *coca*, she made a slew of them for our wedding. I'll never forget how I spotted Philippe's grand-parents, who speak no English, talking over *coca* slices to our American family and friends, who spoke no French but had flown to France for the wedding. The conversation—animated and full of laughter—transcended spoken language. While I couldn't hear exactly what they were saying, a mix of French and English and a lot of pantomimed charade moves kept the discussion alive. And all because a bunch of Americans wanted to thank Mamy for making something delicious for them to eat. That's the uniting power of family recipes being shared across generations and across borders.

Recipes and food connect us to family present and past. I think of my grandma every time I make that German rouladen, a classic dish of thinly sliced beef rolled up around a pickle filling and braised. And I smile when I'm served a weak cup of coffee, which is exactly how she liked her brew: "a product of the Great Depression," she would always say. At Christmastime, the grocery store displays of the holiday candy Almond Roca remind me of how she liked to eat it year-round, so I'd always hunt for suppliers and stock up extra in December to get her at least through March.

And diners always make me think of Grandma. For years, Grandma ate dinner at Polly's Pies every Tuesday. Her order was half a tuna salad sandwich and a side of coleslaw. She'd say, "Always eat raw cabbage when you have the chance." She claimed it was the healthiest food on the planet and, according to her, the reason she lived well into her nineties. When she died, the reception after her funeral was held at Polly's Pies, where many of us ordered "The Ursula" in her memory. Even the manager had kind words to share about serving my grandma over the years, reinforcing the notion that shared meals over time take on deep and resonant meaning.

How Food Connects Us to God's Providence

Discovering Mom's recipe box gave me more than just a connection to my past. It also showed me God's providence and perfect timing. I'd grown up eating Mom's simple dishes, so it came as no surprise to see by her recipes that she wasn't an amazing chef. But somehow I'd just assumed her cooking efforts were a function of limited time and money. After all, she'd been a single mom as well as a full-time college and then medical student for most of my childhood. But I wonder what would have happened if I'd discovered earlier that Mom truly wasn't an accomplished cook. Would I have pursued a career doing something that I clearly had no natural genetic disposition or natural talent for? For whatever reason, her treasured, unambitious recipe box came to me long after it was too late for me to turn back: I'd already spent several seasons creating *Ten Dollar Dinners* on Food Network, and I'd already published my first cookbook. My mom's work was already done. I became the cook she would never be, not in spite of but maybe even because of the woman she was—and because of God's timing.

I believe my mom's heart influenced me way more than her skills in the kitchen. Turns out the work and care of preparing food for others is as important as the food itself, perhaps more so. Those we welcome to our tables care far more about our welcome than what we offer them on their plates.

Maybe you consider yourself an average cook who doesn't order exotic spices from online purveyors or make meals that look like they came from a Michelin-starred restaurant. Perhaps you even face 5:00 p.m. on a Tuesday with a certain amount of dread and then decide to whip up a trusty meat loaf while your children roll their eyes. I'd like to offer some encouragement. Keep cooking. Keep feeding those you love, and keep sharing food with new friends. Keep inviting friends, family, and strangers to your table and serve them the weird Libby Dips of the world. We are all made richer and better and closer to God when we eat one another's food.

Also, write down the recipes you use even if you think they're simple or boring. Your cooking—your legacy—matters more than you know.

RSVP to the Invitation into Connection

- Be intentional about creating your culinary legacy. Put together a family recipe book even if you aren't a big cook. Ask relatives for any family recipes they might have. And don't forget your own additions! Ask your family about their favorite dishes and include those recipes in your family's culinary legacy.
- In Matthew 10:42, Jesus said, "If anyone gives even a cup of cold water to one of these little ones who is my disciple, truly I tell you, that person will certainly not lose their reward." If sharing cool water with a thirsty disciple is reward-worthy, what does that say about sharing even our simplest meals with our family? Reconsider the beauty in even the most basic meals, whether made by you or made for you.
- In addition to gathering recipes, consider creating some mealtime traditions that celebrate connection. Maybe make it a tradition to have everyone share the high point of their day at the dinner table. Or perhaps it's a weekly or monthly tradition to host potlucks with family friends or families new to the neighborhood. In what ways can you turn your family's food memories into relationship memories?

Chapter 8

Feeding the Ones We Love

An Invitation into Nurturing

Feeding others gives us a peek
into how much God wants to
nurture us through food.

Loving our families and friends gives us a glimpse of God's love for us, and feeding them helps us understand how God lovingly uses food to nurture us. Families are not just a matter of birth and blood. Jesus called his disciples "brothers," defined his followers as family, and showed us in the book of John that true love is about service and action. In John 13, Jesus commanded us to love one another "as I have loved you" (verse 34). As a single woman during my twenties and thirties, my girlfriends were family. Then, as newlyweds, Philippe and I were part of a deeply connected group of friends who shared a meal together weekly. We cook for the people in our communities out of a deep love and an innate desire to nurture one another.

In this chapter, though, my stories will be a lot more about my children because they're who I see around my table every day. But the call to feed others is for all of us, parents or not. For me, having children helped me better understand God's love for us as our Father. Being a mom also helped me accept the unconditional nature of God's love for us and the wisdom of his rebukes. Feeding my own family also gave me insight into how deeply God wants to nurture us through the food he created. Finally, all relationships require selflessness and nurture, and even a simple pan of shared lasagna can communicate that kind of love.

Nurturing the Mom

When I was pregnant with Valentine, I planned to breastfeed her once she was born, and I looked forward to the connection that nourishing my new baby would create. But even great plans get derailed. We also planned for a natural childbirth, using a method called hypnobirthing. Philippe and I spent weeks taking classes with a hypnobirthing coach where I learned how to meditate on pleasant birthing thoughts as soft music played (my favorite prerecorded mantra: "The tissue of my birth canal is soft and pink"). We were blissfully happy, awaiting the medicine-free, peaceful arrival of our first child. Even her arrival was a story of the nurturing power of feeding others and allowing others to nourish me.

Twelve days after my due date, the doctor scheduled an induction for January 11. Medical induction wasn't what we'd hoped for and not at all what we'd envisioned. My doctor told me to be at the hospital at midnight. I sensed right away that my plans and careful preparation were mostly theoretical at this point. Something way bigger than me was taking over. It was time to buckle up for the ride.

Almost as if he knew I would need strength for the journey, Philippe surprised me early that evening by making my very favorite meal. He bought us huge, gorgeous steaks—a rare treat on our meager student budget—and cooked them exactly the way I love beef: red but warm; in that very small window between medium-rare and rare. It's hard to get it truly perfect, and I was touched that he had. Even better, he had the recorded finale of our favorite show, *The Amazing Race*, ready and waiting. A perfect date to calm my nerves before heading to the hospital to get hooked up to a Pitocin drip and become a mom.

Just as we cued up the TiVo (this was 2005) and settled in with over-flowing plates, the hospital called. Philippe answered. I could hear the voice through the receiver. There'd been a change in scheduling and they could accommodate us sooner, so did we want to come right away? We faced a choice: meet our baby a few hours earlier, or stay to enjoy Philippe's amazing dinner and find out which team would win the million dollars? I chose to enjoy the gift of the food. We'd be parents forever, so really what was a few extra hours of waiting? We ate the dinner and watched the finale, and I went to the hospital feeling loved, strong, and ready. That is the power of a meal made with love—and good television.

Despite all our planning and our dreams of a hypnobirth, the word *labor* lived up to the name. If you haven't given birth to kids, let me tell you, labor is hard—and for all the effort you put forth for hours, you get ice chips for sustenance. Seriously? About ten hours in, I started losing my enthusiasm and good humor about the project, and I gently nudged my face away from the plastic cup of ice chips that Philippe offered me. (If he were writing this, he might use the words *threw the cup of ice chips across the room,* but he's given to embellishment, and when he writes his own book, well, then it will be time for his version.) But perfect, wonderful Philippe kept his cool and gave me a look that told me he was up to something. He went to his parka and pulled out of the pocket a small sandwich he had made just in case. "I know you get low blood sugar." (That's code for "You're cranky when you're hungry.") I don't know if I've ever been so in love with my husband as I was in that moment. He sneaked me a tiny bite of the PB&J every half hour to help me keep up my energy for this round-the-clock athletic event. Sneaking in a peanut butter sandwich is the stuff of Jesus-level love. At least it felt that way to me.

When the doctor said the baby's heart rate was dropping and he needed to deliver her immediately by cesarean section, I was ready to trade in my hypnobirthing baby dream for an actual baby who was safe and healthy. They upped the epidural (which I had asked for after eight or nine hours), and everyone waited for its effects to kick in, testing with pinpricks on my thigh. I felt those pricks, so they gave me a full spinal block even though it would mean not walking for hours after the birth. The nurses prepped me for surgery and draped the curtain that saved my face from the behind-the-scenes view of a C-section birth. Still, I felt the pinpricks. "Is it possibly a phantom feeling since you can see us poking?" the nurse wanted to know. I closed my eyes. I felt the pricks. I was sure of it. Wasn't I? I was confused and tired, and I knew my baby needed to get out, and I conceded that it was certainly *possible* that I was wrong.

I was not wrong. The instant the surgery began, that became clear. What I witnessed next will forever amaze me. The entire medical team sprang into action as the head doctor loudly but calmly called out a new emergency protocol. What unfolded was like a well-rehearsed Thursday night episode of *ER,* and everyone knew their part. Someone grabbed my husband and kicked him out of the operating room. With no time for explanation, he thought I was dying. Then, in fewer than two seconds of excruciating pain, I saw a dark gray mask racing toward my face. My last thought was that I needed to confess eating half a sandwich, but I had no time.

I woke up groggy and confused, unable to move any part of my body, drool caked on my cheek. *Did we have a baby?* They brought in my sweet husband, whose face I instantly read as exhausted, and his eyes were red and puffy from tears of panic and fear, mixed with relief and deep joy. He was holding our tiny, wrinkly baby, who was edgy from the drama of being yanked from the womb and was still nameless. This wasn't the seeing-my-child-for-the-first-time moment I had imagined. I'd never seen this in a movie. No one told me to push one last time because they could see the shoulders. No one gave us our "It's a girl!" moment. And I was immobile, and the baby was crying, and in my daze I had to be told twice that we had a daughter. But the three of us together made a new unit, a family. I got my first, tiny glimpse into the intense kind of love God must have for us.

Even after a harrowing twenty-four hours, I insisted that the breastfeeding dream still lived on. There was no price too high to pay for this little person, and my heart willed away the anesthesia so I could feed her. I was hardwired to feed Valentine, not just to fill her tummy but to surround her with love and let her know she wasn't alone—that she would never be alone on this path called life. This gift of mother's milk was more than physical nourishment; it was nurture and comfort and a tiny example of the deep, full love I had for her. It was my very best gift to her, and I wanted her to want it. I knew in my soul that God felt the same way about us, and this immediately drew me closer to him.

Breastfeeding may be natural, but it's not easy, and Valentine's stressful beginnings left us both weary from trying to learn our new skill. I felt like a failure, both at birthing and as a mom, and I spent four emotional days in the hospital trying to get us back on the new-mommy track I had seen in movies. Recovery was slow for us both—and for good reason. The nurses explained that the surgery had been quick and rough in their attempt to get Valentine out in the seconds-long window between my being knocked out and the anesthesia reaching her. Sometimes she would wear her "I'm a Hypnobirthing Baby" onesie, a prelabor gift from our coach, and I would either laugh or cry depending on the whims of my shifting hormones.

We plugged along, determined to put what was best for the baby above everything else. I breastfed for several months, clumsily, neither of us ever getting the hang of it, despite the help of fantastic books and lactation consultants. When a very probreastfeeding leader of a La Leche League meeting gently invited me to *stop* breastfeeding, I was relieved. Nurturing my baby would look different from my preparenting imagination. Valentine was three months old, and it turned out that I was pregnant already with Charlotte. With months of morning sickness awaiting just around the corner, I was grateful for formula: it changed our feeding routine from tense to pleasurable. Finally, I could nurture Valentine through food in peace.

Charlotte was born almost exactly a year after Valentine in the kind of planned C-section where I emerged still freshly showered from being at home merely an hour or two earlier and even wearing a little makeup. No sneaked-in sandwich was needed. My desire to breastfeed Charlotte was just as fierce as it had been for Valentine. I found my own rhythm of breastfeeding Charlotte while spooning mushy baby food into Valentine's mouth. It felt like my entire existence centered around either giving these two babies food or cleaning up the resulting diapers afterward. Charlotte is famous in family lore as being the easiest baby possible, and there is no question in my mind why God did this. He knew our family wasn't complete, and with two babies in diapers, I needed a small boost of Mommy-confidence to consider having a third baby. I was managing two babies, and I felt like a rock star. Adding a third baby would be a piece of cake.

Valentine wasn't even two and Charlotte was ten months old the day we found out I was pregnant—with twins. We didn't even have to ask: we knew the twins would be girls, and we couldn't have been more thrilled. And we were chill. Handling two babies in diapers will do that to you. We were so chill that when my water started trickling at thirty-three weeks, I didn't even bother Philippe at work because I knew he had an important meeting that day. I called my next-door neighbor Jade who had mentioned she was heading to Costco that day, which was a block away from the hospital. I handed my babies to another neighbor and, sitting on towels to protect her leather seats, caught a ride with Jade and her toddler. When I arrived at the maternity ward and my water broke in a big way in the hallway (finally a real movie moment!), the nurses asked me if I was alone. When I explained that a neighbor had dropped me off on her way to Costco, they exchanged the briefest of looks. *Your water broke, and your friend went to Costco?* Yeah, perhaps I'd gotten a little too chill.

Philippe arrived, and we had the babies that very day. They stayed in the NICU, where I learned a whole new world of feeding that involved feeding tubes and "kangaroo time," where you hold the baby against your bare skin so they connect with you. It's proven to help babies grow, the nurses told me. I cherished this time, because these teeny little preemie babies were just the snuggliest, softest little beings I'd ever touched. I'm not sure who was nurturing whom then.

Margaux, Océane, and Charlotte all breastfed with no problem (well, a more normal level of problems), which allowed me to understand something important about my mothering: I fed our babies differently but with the same love and intention. And that held true as they got older: Valentine started solid foods while I was super pregnant with Charlotte, and I served her prepared baby food that I bought on sale at Target. Charlotte bypassed most of the soft-rice-cereal phase entirely after the night she reached over, grabbed pieces of Valentine's pizza, and stuffed them into her gummy, toothless mouth. She never looked back, and I don't blame her. Pizza is good, wise child.

The twins may have the ideal early food story: I made every last bite of their food, blending up fresh vegetables and fruit and filling ice-cube trays with organic homemade baby purees. They ate every veggie I could find and even downed without complaint healthy things like brewer's-yeast-and-millet cereal I concocted. I tasted every single recipe I made for the girls, and I can confirm that some of them tasted too healthy—sometimes downright yucky—for my own palate. But the twins didn't mind. They ate whatever their mom or their sisters gave them. Valentine and Charlotte helped me make their baby sisters' food, standing on chairs pulled up to the kitchen island. I think that by helping make their sisters' food, they fell deeper in love with them.

Hidden Gifts in Feeding Kids

Feeding family and friends has always been one of my love languages, but feeding this new family required a new level of commitment and energy. Orchestrating the various food needs for four babies of different ages was a big part of those early days. All four girls loved how much time we spent in the kitchen. The first word for two of my daughters was *cheese*. We loved to cook and eat and create. The girls could tear lettuce for my salad before they could walk. But we were also on a budget, now with six mouths to feed and still on one income. I expanded my baby-food making into yogurt making. I discovered that every morning the dairy aisle of my local supermarket would mark down milk that had fewer than three days on the "Sell By" date. So I started planning my shopping trips for just after nine o'clock, and I'd scoop up a couple of gallons of organic whole milk marked to half price with big orange stickers. I'd use a few tablespoons of plain yogurt as a starter, whisk it into gently heated milk, and then pour it into large mason jars, which I'd stick in my hot Texas garage overnight. Voilà! I had gorgeous organic yogurt for pennies on the dollar.

My girls all loved yogurt. I calculated that I was saving well over a hundred dollars a month just by making my own. Watching the girls eat my homemade yogurt was a joy. The yogurt made us all feel loved—them for my making it, and me for their eating it. I imagine that God intentionally gave food this power.

But therein lies the risk in being the nurturer: sometimes the recipient isn't as grateful as we'd hoped. I know for a fact that God has given me a lot of gifts that I have not received graciously or that I have outright rejected. My kids did the same thing. They definitely weren't always grateful and willing to eat my healthy offerings. Feeding a family as a parent shed light on what God must feel like when we are ungrateful. Out of four daughters, two (and a half?) ended up being picky eaters. I was frustrated by my kids who'd barely touch a roasted potato because there was a piece of green rosemary on it. The bigger sadness was for how much of God's gift they were refusing daily. So I searched and researched. Much of what was out there on picky eating just made me feel guilty. There is a common, simplified narrative that assumes that a child's pickiness is a result of lazy or bad parenting. While I am far from perfect, I am a pretty purposeful parent who reads labels, limits sugary foods, and cooks with my kids. I never let the kids load up on juice or sodas, and I didn't let them snack on junk. After all, I'm a professional cook on television! My babies ate flax and lentils and brewer's yeast! But, still, the pickiness came.

I suspected it wasn't just one but rather many issues that played into their picky eating. Research confirmed this. I was relieved to discover that I wasn't just a crummy parent and that I wasn't failing at my call to nurture my kids and love them well. As it turns out there are many reasons, such as a physiological difference in taste (kids' taste buds perceive taste differently, and little Margaux turned out to be a supertaster); a lack of nutritional context (would I eat broccoli as often if I didn't understand its benefits?); power assertions (kids learn very young that one of the few things they do have control over is their swallow mechanism, so can we blame them for wanting to exercise it?); negative associations or experiences with certain foods (I still get the willies thinking about the time a relative wouldn't let me leave the table until I finished an old glass of milk); habits (what is the easiest snack option in the household, and does it promote healthy eating?); and just plain exhaustion (ever try to get a two-year-old who has missed a nap to eat a veggie?). So if you have picky kiddos, take heart in knowing you aren't alone.

The list of reasons why kids are picky felt overwhelming, but the girls were missing out on the delight, connection, and love of our Maker. I decided to create my own program for them. I developed activities and exercises to counteract each one of the root causes. This wasn't about getting the kids to choke down a few bites of cauliflower; I wanted to shift the needle in a deeper way, to nurture them better through the food God has given us. I wanted the girls to have a positive long-term relationship with food and to see it as the invitation from God that it is.

This wasn't something we could fix with a magical spinach recipe that all kids would love. We needed to address the deeper stuff behind the pickiness. I created an entire program to help reorient my kids' palates and address the root causes, and the result was *The Picky Eaters Project* web series I did for Food Network. My experiment worked. Helping my girls address their pickiness helped them connect with people, history, the earth, and God. When my girls move out of my home one day (like when they are thirty, I've decided), I hope they enter the world fully equipped to continue a lifelong love and respect for the relationship between food and their bodies and the God who made them because I took the time to nourish them. Ultimately, they are on God's journey. I'm grateful I get to be the one shepherding them and feeding them now on his behalf. However much I love them, I know he loves them even more.

Feeding family and friends is one way to celebrate the nurturer that God wove into all of us. Cooking for our neighbor who just had a baby, creating a supper club that meets monthly, or even making spaghetti on a Tuesday night for our kids are all expressions of our care and love. Our experience with picky eating informed my own response to God's nurturing gifts and to food in particular. When I'm tempted to open the fridge and complain because I'm tired of leftovers, I hear my own entitlement a little more clearly. Becoming a nurturer developed in me a greater sense of gratitude for food.

RSVP to the Invitation into Nurturing

- God nurtures us through food. Isaiah 25:6 describes the messianic banquet: "On this mountain the LORD Almighty will prepare a feast of rich food for all peoples, a banquet of aged wine—the best of meats and the finest of wines." So many of us are tasked with cooking or preparing food for others. The next time you make a meal or dish for someone, pause for a moment and pray for that person. Intentionally thinking about who eats the food you make will change the way you cook.

- Think of the last time someone made you food, even if it was at a restaurant. For a moment, imagine each person involved in the delivery of that food to your fork as being the earthly hands and feet of God, bringing you nourishment. Take just one dish and pray to God with thanksgiving for every tiny bit of nurture that came through an entire supply chain of people—from the farmer to the truck driver to the store clerk to the cook to you.

- Everyone who has cooked for someone picky knows the frustration of preparing a lovely homemade meal only to have it shunned for a chicken nugget. I want to shout to my kids: Don't turn down a gorgeous roasted chicken, potatoes, and root veggies meal for a greasy, sodium-laden, processed nugget! But I wonder if we do the same with God. What valuable idea of God's might you be shunning in favor of a salty, fatty nugget because it tastes good in the short term?

Chapter 9

Ten Dollar Dinners

An Invitation into Stewardship

Stewards are entrusted servants,
not owners.

When I started the show *Ten Dollar Dinners,* friends and fans nodded at the idea of a budget-conscious cooking show. I heard repeatedly how smart it was in "these economic times" to find such a marketable angle. But *Ten Dollar Dinners* wasn't about buying the cheapest ingredient I could find to fill a tummy and scarfing it down. It was, for me, a celebration of our resources—from finances to time to earth resources. I wanted to celebrate the natural seasons of food that God has given us. *Ten Dollar Dinners* was never just about frugality; it was about spending with purpose, being mindful, shopping well, and choosing to buy according to God's rhythms. It was about dependence on God and gratitude for his gifts. *Ten Dollar Dinners* was about stewardship.

Eating any food is, by definition, an act of participating in God's creation and its system of life and death. How we eat determines whether we are helping or harming his creation; it determines if the death is redemptive. Knowing more about the price that a creature paid for the easy delivery of food onto our plates shouldn't scare us or even annoy us because it's God's invitation to stay closer to his food, to his creation. And it's an opportunity to be closer to God, to be mindful of our connection to him and to one another. We are privy to receiving God's best when we step into the role he created for us: stewards of his creation.

Rethinking the Idea of Stewardship

When you hear someone mention stewardship, do you immediately think of the church's annual fund-raising season? I grew up hearing about the importance of giving our time, talents, and treasures to the church, which is a nice way of asking us to grab our checkbooks or credit cards. While stewardship *is* about giving money, it's about something much deeper.

The creation story in Genesis clearly tells us that our stewardship of God's earth is foundational: God made people to work on his earth and take care of it. Genesis 2:15 says, "The LORD God took the man and put him in the Garden of Eden to work it and take care of it." What God has given us isn't ours to *use up;* it's ours to *care for.* God is the owner; we are the caregivers: "The earth is the LORD's, and everything in it, the world, and all who live in it" (Psalm 24:1). The implications go far beyond managing a food budget and making prudent purchases. It goes beyond what my mom taught me about managing and making do with what we have.

At the heart of stewardship is gratitude: it's acknowledging the generosity of God and honoring him by treating his creation and his gifts to us with respect and care. That means we are mindful not just of how much we spend on our food, but that our food system comprises sources that also honor God and his creation. And the very heart of stewardship goes all the way back to who we are.

We are part of God's creation as well as participants in the complex system God designed, which deliberately connects us to one another in many ways, including through food. We are literally creatures in his world, and we are part of a rich web of other creatures and creations, including tall giraffes, tiny ladybugs, slippery dolphins, sweet baby puppies, stinky skunks, woolly sheep, flowy willow trees, soaring palm trees, prickly cacti, tiny forest mushrooms, and microbes living in the rich soil that sustains it all. We eat plants and animals fed by plants and other animals supported by this soil, and all creatures give back to the soil through excretion and, ultimately, death. In his brilliant and rich book *Food and Faith,* Norman Wirzba refers to us all as "members" of God's creation. Food powerfully binds us together. Right there in Genesis we are invited to participate in creation as the shepherds of the earth.

Not only are we members of God's creation, but we are special members because God put us in charge. But when God says that we are created to "rule over" his creation, he is handing us stewardship, not ownership (Genesis 1:26). We are quite literally God's mini-mes: we are called to love the earth as he does and, by doing so, honor him, the delighted Creator who molded us from dust.

Since "ruling over" is not ownership, it is also not license to do whatever we want; it's not an invitation to exploit. Stewardship is an invitation to care for. When the kids were younger, we had an au pair living with us. When my husband and I would leave the kids with her, they understood that in our absence, the au pair was our proxy. She was "ruling over" them. She had my blessing to make decisions on my behalf in my absence. Her assignment was to prioritize the well-being of my precious creations while their father and I were away. Still, the kids actually belonged to us, not to her. She had to give them back at the end of the night and in as close to their original shape as possible.

As much as I love my kiddos, God loves his creation and his creatures more.

We are creation's caregivers, and an important part of that care is how we treat and sustain the aspects of the creation that provide us food. We owe God the care of his earth and the animals that feed us. And just like an au pair, we are called to honor the original artist's masterpieces. The au pair would be a horrible babysitter if she spent her time texting her friends and watching YouTube while she was supposed to be watching my daughters. Similarly, we are not off the hook simply because we are so busy fulfilling our desire to make a profit—and have the cheapest food possible—that we shield our eyes from the impact of our own selfishness. When we put on blinders to shield our conscience, we cannot with legitimacy claim ignorance about the food system. If we prioritize money, ease, and comfort above all else, we cannot face our Maker at the end of our lives and say we did our best with his earth. How we choose to respond to our stewardship responsibilities matters.

A Closer Look at God's Food System

Caring for creation isn't easy. It's joyous and it's good, but it's hard. It's tough to think about an animal dying for us to eat a casual Tuesday dinner. My friend and fellow *Guy's Grocery Games* judge Duskie Estes, who happens to be one of the best chefs I know, is also a pig farmer and amazing mom. Duskie believes in the one-bad-day philosophy of raising pigs: they are pets until the moment they are not. And then their death is beautifully redeemed by using every last bit of the pig's sacrifice.

One day in the makeup trailer of *Guy's Grocery Games,* Duskie told us all that when it was age appropriate, she invited her daughters to witness the slaughter of one of their pigs. To commemorate the event, the girls stitched together their own purses out of the pigskin. "If you can't watch how the meat is made, then you haven't earned the right to eat its body" is her philosophy. Whoa. That seems intense. But Duskie's way seems to be the right way. It seems fair that we shouldn't take for granted the sacrifice of a fellow member of creation.

I don't believe we're responsible for making the entire ecosystem death-free. I'm not even sure if that is what God would want or what the implications would be. But in God's economy, deaths are redemptive and we should honor that. Death is meant to matter, not to become a meaningless habit of entitlement. Casually eating a chicken thigh without pausing to consider what has happened before is arrogant and not fitting for someone who is entrusted to be a steward of the chicken in the first place. That God allows us to eat what once was alive does not absolve us of our responsibility to nurture life. In fact, it makes our responsibility all the more relevant.

We owe the Maker of creation our earnest attention and care for the members that we consume. Through food we connect ourselves in an intimate, deep way with the rest of creation. Our bodies are currently absorbing the nutrients from the soil that grew the veggies that we ate last night for dinner. When we serve a lamb roast at a dinner party, our guests are all taking into their bodies that lamb, its DNA and its history. Today, I ate a Thai chicken salad from Trader Joe's and saw that it was made in Monrovia, California. I sat for a moment and wondered, *Who are the others who are sharing the same exact chicken with me today?*

On a practical level, we can't personally meet every creature that will grace our table. Life is busy and modern. However, we have separated ourselves so far from food as it exists in its natural, God-given state that when my own kids—children of a mom who makes her living in food!—were younger, they didn't even realize that chicken-in-a-package was the same thing as chicken-on-a-farm, so little did they resemble one another. When Valentine was seven and she discovered that our Thanksgiving turkey was a creature, she shunned it completely. She announced to her three little sisters at the table that the golden, perfectly brined turkey on the platter in front of us was an actual animal (masterful pause for effect) "and it's *dead*." (We had a lot of tears and leftovers that year.) But Valentine brought up a fair concern. When we associate food more closely with man-made machinery and manipulation than we do with God's gift and provision, we are more than irresponsible stewards—we are missing out on intimacy with creation. And so stewardship calls for prudence.

Making Good Decisions About Our Food

Managing our financial resources is good stewardship. A wise budget-shopper is a flexible one who is willing to buy the vegetables that are in season for the dinner menu. Doing so not only keeps us in line with God's rhythms but also saves us money. Yet prudence isn't just about thrift. It's about weighing the choices and making the wisest, most benevolent one. I used to buy the very cheapest chicken breasts I could find without giving any thought to the life of the chicken before it showed up sanitized and sealed in plastic packaging. Recently I realized how naive this was. I was assuming that my fellow humans would treat animals in ways consistent with God's calling. I didn't know that there were chickens being overfed to the point of not being able to walk under the weight of their overgrown bodies. But the simple truth is, if I find white-meat chicken for a buck-fifty a pound, it begs the question: How much money could have possibly been spent raising it? I didn't know about these inhumanely treated creatures, but my ignorance was not benevolent innocence. I should have known. I was essentially being the babysitter who put on earphones with blaring music, blotting out the cries of the children she is caring for.

Now I make my budget meals still happen by being extra diligent to stock up and freeze when free-range meat is on sale. I am also more flexible about including meat as a side, not the main source of calories on my family's plate. Serving less meat allows me to keep our food budget down while also allowing me to buy meat I can feel better about as both a caregiver to my family and a steward of God's creation.

There is grace for what we do in ignorance. But we aren't to willfully turn our heads the other way and choose to ignore truth in order to be held accountable to a lower standard. God is smarter than that, and he deserves our willingness to take on the responsibility and accountability for creation care.

Stewardship includes the responsibility to make prudent decisions, not just about the money we spend at the store but also about *all* of the food system, including the treatment of animals, sustainability, and environmental impact. I'm mindful now of the lives lost and the agricultural practices used in the food system life cycle.

"What would Jesus do?" turns out to be an excellent question to consider when we think about how we approach everything from our weekly food budget to our food system. How would Jesus treat animals before they are slaughtered? As Duskie mentioned, are these animals having only one bad day or a lifetime of misery? And how should knowing how the animals are treated affect what we choose to pay for and eat? Would Jesus offer fair wages to workers in the field even if it meant consumers paid a few cents more per pound of tomatoes? We owe it to the creatures and the creation in our care to not pillage the earth in pursuit of our own goals. We owe it to our Creator to care for his creation; it was actually the first thing he ever asked us to do.

Stewarding Well What We Spend on Our Food

One of the unexpected gifts of being raised on a tight budget was the lack of processed foods available to us. Mom kept granola bars in her purse for hunger emergencies (some things about parenting never change), but it was understood that they were for true food crises, not for casual nibbling out of boredom while waiting in line at the bank. Also, since my family was always on a tight budget, overspending wasn't a temptation for me while I was growing up.

My mom was a master at stretching a dollar. She proudly bought chicken wings for thirty-five cents a pound, long before chicken wings were a popular bar food. Back then, the wings were just Z-shaped pieces of the chicken's body that were awkward to eat, requiring us to navigate around all the chicken skin and bones to access a few nibbles of actual meat. It seemed inefficient to me, even then, but Mom knew wings to be a thrifty choice since no one wanted to bother with eating them, and that price was a dealmaker for her. Mom grew squash and tomatoes in the Arizona heat of our backyard, and we gathered eggs each day from our large flock of chickens (and this was long before backyard chickens were a thing). If this sounds like we lived on some kind of desert farm, know that we absolutely did not. We lived right in the city limits of Tucson in a tiny A-frame stucco house with a small backyard—half concrete slab and half dirt dried hard in the heat, with a few sprigs of desert grasses poking out.

Mom's meal repertoire was well intentioned, but limited, as were her cooking skills. Scrambled eggs were a common meal, served with homegrown tomatoes we held in our hands and ate whole like apples. It never occurred to me to slice a tomato until I was well into my teens. Though she wasn't a talented cook, Mom was a genius at using inexpensive ingredients to stretch expensive ones: she made tacos using cheap, chopped potatoes studded with just enough ground beef to reasonably call them "beef tacos." Sometimes she would slather inexpensive grape jelly right onto salted hot fried corn tortillas and call them "tostadas." Fridays, she served baked fish—not because we were Catholic but because Mom's repertoire was probably seven dishes long—and her famous lemon-buttered potatoes, which had exactly zero actual butter in them. "Real butter is for rich people," Mom would say wistfully, full of hope and expectation that one day she herself might purchase and serve butter. (She did.) Other items reserved for rich people, according to Mom, were olive oil, string cheese, half-and-half, and paper napkins.

So I come by my bargain-cooking roots naturally. I'm physically unable to purchase an item at the grocery store without checking the price. I often dazzle my kids (well, maybe just mildly entertain them) with my uncanny ability to predict our grocery bill with astonishing accuracy. As we place an item on the conveyor belt, I let the girls know its price—already impressing them with my great memory of the price posted on the shelf—and we add it all up in our heads, tack on tax, and make our final guesses before the cashier announces the total. I daresay that price recall is a bit of a superpower of mine. I'm confident that anytime my guess is off from the totals, it's due to a calculation error, not a lack of price awareness. I am the customer who follows the prices as they post on the register screen and notices the grapes that are on sale for $1.99 a pound rang up at $3.99.

Furthermore, I am incapable of buying something when I don't know the price. In restaurants where the server recites the daily specials, I always nicely inquire about the price even if I have zero intention of ordering it. I do this purely on principle, hoping to remove the apparent stigma attached to wanting to know the price of the items we agree to purchase. It is absurd to expect consumers to buy something without knowing the bill they will be expected to pay. I have spent too much time in restaurants inwardly calculating whether I could afford to add the side salad to my meal. Restaurant dish prices vary tremendously, especially when it comes to the daily specials, and leaving the prices out of a rich description that has everyone's mouths watering seems to imply that if you have to ask the price, then you don't belong there. It seems unkind.

My mindfulness with money has its roots in the years when I truly had to calculate how much my grocery bill would be because I was on such a tight budget that an extra two bucks in grapes was a luxury I couldn't afford. And before that, I had often stood at the register with my mom as she asked the cashier to void a few items from the grocery order so she could afford to pay for the remainder of the bill. It's amazing how accurately you can add in your head when your dignity depends on it.

So, stewardship is a calling to care—about our budgets, our earth, our families, our plants, and our fellow creatures on this planet. Saving money is part of stewardship, yet it is but a tiny peek into the deeper calling to be mindful members of our creation. We don't all have to be vegetarians like Valentine, but we do have the responsibility to own our role as the head of the food system. And when we sit down to eat a meal—whether it's a gorgeous plate of grilled vegetables or a perfectly pink roast beef—we owe our Creator, and his creation, the gratitude and care worthy of His gifts that feed us.

Take a simple dish like my quiche with onion and fennel. It's not just an easy recipe for a weeknight dinner; it's a small miracle! You know this if you've ever tried to grow onions and fennel. Chickens laying eggs that we can eat is pretty darned cool, too, if you think about it. And the crust for this quiche, made of butter and flour and baked into flaky perfection? Also a mini-miracle. Eating mindlessly blinds us to these miracles, which are really quite incredible little gifts from God. Which means we are missing out on intimacy with our Creator—which is missing out on the very reason we were created.

The good news is, the reverse is also true. We can be closer to God when we care for his creation and when we pay attention to what we eat, how we eat it, and how it was produced. When we stay close to our creation and take care of it, we are living with gratitude and giving God the glory he deserves for our creative, complicated, wonderfully delicious, and miraculous food.

RSVP to the Invitation into Stewardship

- Think about the last meal you ate and two or three of the ingredients in one of the dishes. Consider how the history of those ingredients affects you. How did those ingredients get to your plate? Did they come from a farm? What might have grown near the ingredients? What would the impact of the soil, the water, and the sun have been on the food? How does it feel knowing that food is in your body? Choose one of the ingredients and do your best to track down its history. Start by asking your grocer. Between the phone and internet, my kids have been able to trace the histories of a number of our ingredients!

- Borrow something valuable from a friend for a day or two. Notice how you take care of it. Do you give it more or less care than you give your own belongings? Why?

- The first job ever given to mankind was to take care of the earth. Genesis 2:15 says, "The Lord God took the man and put him in the Garden of Eden to work it and take care of it." Make a list of things that we prioritize over caring for God's earth, things such as convenience, money, and time. If God himself were here managing our food decisions, in what ways do you think he would have you do things differently? What changes—in food or otherwise—can you make to better care for God's creation?

Chapter 10

The Downside of Foodie Culture

An Invitation into Humility

Foodie culture may be chipping
away at God's food culture.

owe my job to the foodie craze of the past two decades that led to the
proliferation of food media outlets, including Food Network, of
course. (Or did Food Network lead the trend? Probably a little of both.)
My work there has put me among a lot of food personalities, voices, and
points of view. Clearly, society has a food obsession, and the fallout has
been both good and bad. On one hand, our foodie culture has brought
us closer to the food that eluded many before it appeared nightly on the
television screen and in our Instagram feeds. In other words, the foodie
culture demystified cooking. Many people tell me they learned to cook
thanks to Food Network shows! But some of the fallout is less desirable
and perhaps even dangerous. I wonder what Jesus thinks of our current
food culture with its Pinterest pictures, diets that vilify food groups,

food identities that presume a certain level of affluence, or the notion that a meal is, at its best, a performance instead of a humble sharing of God-given gifts. And what does Jesus think of "food porn"?

I became acutely aware of this cultural tension during my many hours in a white, unmarked fifteen-passenger van. Riding in such a vehicle is not glamorous, by any stretch of the imagination, and it turns out to be a pretty equalizing experience. Maybe that's why, as *The Next Food Network Star* contestants, we were transported around in this van to all of our weekly challenges. We spent hours in that van, which always smelled like a mix of sunflower seed shells and old Sprite. Whether we drove to the Food Network studios just a few blocks away from our carriage house, or headed out of town to cook at Ina Garten's house in the Hamptons, our trusty van was what got us there. We'd laugh, talk, and swap stories of our lives at home. Michael kept us laughing with stories about his quirky mom, Betty. Debbie shared about her life growing up in a Korean family, and Jen, a newlywed, told us about her wedding. As the competition wore on, sometimes we consoled one another when one of us had bombed a challenge and felt sure of imminent elimination. Our love for food and a shared desire to make it onto Food Network united us.

We also talked a lot about actual food. We had different backgrounds and perspectives, which gave us each a unique voice, and each of us had our expertise to share. Jeffrey knew more about spices than anyone I'd ever met, Eddie taught me about making fritters by deep-frying grocery-store dough from a pop-up can, and Jamika shared her secrets for the best collard greens I've ever tasted. When we talked about food, I felt plugged in and connected. I adored learning the history of my new friends. But when our conversations took a slight turn to discussing the trendy chef scene, I sat quietly, unable to add to the conversation. Sure, I knew all the famous chefs on television, but the cast of characters of the off-screen chef world was foreign to me. Discussions about which chefs owned which restaurants and who had earned James Beard nominations or Michelin stars flew over my head without a backward glance. As a mom of four little ones in diapers, living in a small Texas town, the restaurant decision my husband and I faced on date nights was simple: P. F. Chang's or the Cheesecake Factory.

In those early seasons of *The Next Food Network Star*, we all lived together. By day we cooked side by side for the judges. At night we cooked for one another. Dinner was our chance to try one another's food, and we took this opportunity seriously. My peers cooked as though they were in a restaurant kitchen, using every dish in the kitchen for their *mise en place* (ingredient prep work), trimming down meat to its prettiest portions, not giving one thought to the cleanup or the astonishingly large scraps they tossed. They firmly flexed their culinary muscles, pulling out their silver-bullet dishes they thought best expressed why they should win.

It never occurred to me to try to impress my fellow contestants because, frankly, I didn't have the restaurant chops to do it. That's not false modesty; that's an acknowledgment of fact. But not knowing how to run a restaurant kitchen doesn't invalidate one's voice in the world of food. None of those contestants knew anything about getting dinner on the table for a family of six, which was my specialty. In fact, a few of them admitted they never cooked at home. After a long night of working in a restaurant, they would return home and feed themselves the one thing that didn't require cooking: a bowl of cereal.

When it came my turn to cook dinner for my fellow contestants, I made marinated flank steak and roasted potatoes—my mom's "fancy meal" recipe but considered incredibly simple by pro-chef standards. I was thrilled to have access to the highest quality meat and gorgeous local green onions, full of a grassy onion flavor that made the dish sing. For the first time since my arrival at the competition, I felt like I was at home, hosting friends for a Sunday supper. But as I sat down to dinner with my new friends, family style, I could sense a shift in energy as we gathered around our meal. The typical high fives and dinnertime swapping of late-night restaurant stories didn't happen. It was as if someone had invited their mom to the prom and no one knew how to act. The competition at this point was well underway, tensions were high, and my home-cooked meal fell flat in this crowd of chefs. In that moment I realized that we were not just a group of friends hanging out over a bite. I also saw how big a chasm there is between home hospitality and restaurant cooking.

Don't get me wrong: I love restaurant chefs! I love a fantastic restaurant meal where the chef uses God's ingredients to make temporary, edible works of art, and many of my friends are gifted chefs. Richard Blais, for instance, is a pure genius with ingredients, and I marvel at any plate he puts together. He can use crazy gastronomy to make never-before-seen versions of things like tiny bubbles of creamy ice cream out of *foie gras*. And Richard isn't just brilliant with the fancy stuff. A few years ago, when I took my six-year-old twins to his high-end restaurant Juniper and Ivy, he himself hopped back into the kitchen to whip us up the gooey-est, cheesiest grilled cheese on perfectly buttered bread, crisped just right. He is an artist, and food is his medium. Watching the interplay between God's ingredients and Richard's creative mind is pure joy, and I observe in awe. It's the same feeling I get when I watch a perfectly danced ballet. The beauty of art in motion moves me to big ploppy tears in the best way possible.

But where does this kind of stunning culinary ability leave the home cook who is cobbling together dinner every night for her family or inviting friends over for a casual meal? Making the artistry of a celebrity chef the home cook's standard in hospitality is shortsighted, even damaging. Who said that the main goal in our home kitchens is to have a restaurant-quality dish at every single meal? When we turn our homes into stages and our cooking into stars, we alienate people. We can even scare them out of cooking for others. What a loss it is that anyone would shy away from welcoming people into their home—as God wants and even commands us to do!—because they are fearful of not measuring up to the average Instagram food post. Or if we are confident in the kitchen, we might make the food about ourselves—about impressing others with our great talent, hard work, or skill—and less about the deeper purpose of food: connecting with people, humbly honoring God's gifts, and enjoying with deep thanksgiving. Whether people are afraid to host at all, or inviting people into our homes becomes all about the host, God isn't glorified. So let's not allow the beautiful artistry of restaurant chefs redefine food's original and noble purpose.

Getting Back to the Basics

I cringe when people call me "chef," because it's a title I have not earned. I have never worked in a restaurant, and chefs work extremely hard to earn that title. I honor their system, and just as a teacher wouldn't allow others to call her "doctor" until she has a PhD in her given field, I don't want to appear to have credentials I haven't earned. I have earned other titles—MBA, *New York Times* best-selling author, Mom—and I would bristle if someone casually attributed them to someone who hadn't earned them. It's not the title that matters; it's what we did to get there that does. I admire the hard work of a chef and the path required to get there.

Also, calling me "chef" simply because I make food on television presupposes that the only valid voice in food—or perhaps the most valid voice—is that of a restaurant chef. I don't have to be a chef to have something meaningful and valuable to say about food. In fact, I would argue that the artist's take on food—making something gorgeous, Instagram-worthy, Pinterest-y, or drool-worthy during a television competition or travel-exposé show—is proportionately a much smaller piece of the food puzzle than the daily task of getting a meal on the table to feed our families. The vast majority of our relationship with food has very little to do with the food narrative told by a fancy restaurant, yet the cultural conversation we are currently having about food would suggest otherwise. This is partly why I miss the early days of food television, those "in the kitchen" shows that essentially taught recipes and gave tips for feeding our families. I think they will come back once the luster of shiny food wears off and we realize we are missing the main thing here: God's gift of food.

The shadow of food looms large in our lives, but perhaps not always in the role it was intended to play. Food media can help or it can hurt that disconnect. I meet viewers all the time who tell me that they watched my show on Food Network and were inspired to go out, buy the ingredients, and try a recipe. Some people tell me they never cooked at all before a Food Network show gave them the confidence to try. It's a joy to be a part of opening doors to newcomers whose interest in food is piqued and then nurtured into a deep love for cooking in general or just for making a meal. God delights in our coming together to prepare his food, share it, enjoy it, and connect with one another.

But on the flip side, I've also met self-proclaimed "foodies" who own hundreds of signed cookbooks yet can't recall the last time they actually made a meal. Let us not be tricked into thinking we are cooking simply because we've watched every single episode of *Chopped*. This is the slippery slope of our current foodie culture. As a society, we talk about food and consume food-related content, but we aren't actually cooking. I call that "being food-adjacent."

Food programs started out as simple invitations to buy some ingredients and cook a recipe. But over time we needed to add bells and whistles to satisfy our ever-shrinking attention spans and ever-growing addiction to bigger and better and more dramatic entertainment. So new genres like reality cooking shows and cooking competitions were created, and there's nothing wrong with them . . . until our imperfect human selves get sucked into the fast-paced flashy drama, and suddenly a show that actually teaches us to cook seems elementary and—dare I say—boring. Slowly, cooking shows become more accurately described as eating shows, and home kitchens across America stay pristine and shiny and clean from lack of use. We—who could be cooking—plop down on the couch to watch some food TV while we wait for the pizza to be delivered.

This pattern separates us even more from God's ingredients, the joy of using them to create, and the health benefits of eating them—yet, ironically, all the while, we are identifying ourselves more and more as foodies. When we mistake the sizzle for the steak, we get into trouble. In fact, that may be worse than recognizing we aren't connected to food at all.

I'll be frank and tell you that I've been part of this problem. I didn't mean to be, but the slippery slope sneaked up on me too, and it's easy to contribute my voice to a conversation without stepping back to evaluate whether the conversation makes sense in the first place.

Over the years that I've worked in food, I've made some changes in the way I talk about food. Just as an example, on *Ten Dollar Dinners* I sometimes would tell viewers that this or that dish was easy to prepare but also "restaurant worthy," as if the highest aspiration of any cook is to serve something worthy of a restaurant. As a home-cook-turned-"celebrity chef" on national television, I was inadvertently snubbing the family meals at home that happen all across this beautiful world. Most of us eat the majority of our meals at home, and I've come to celebrate that fact. I'm more careful with my language now, and I honor the food we make daily as much as I do the intricate, artistic meals that get much of the culture's attention.

No-Fear Cooking!

Thanks to both social and traditional media, the standard we hold for the home cook has changed, and the result is a growing fear of cooking for others. Who wants to risk the shame of a total Pinterest fail? Is this fear something you struggle with? Do you ever feel frustrated because what you cook doesn't resemble at all what you see on television or social media? Do you feel nervous about hosting a dinner party? I don't want you to miss out on the gift and joy of preparing food to glorify God simply because you're intimidated by a fancy restaurant or a television show or Pinterest.

Food porn is not a higher calling than receiving and sharing food with humility and thanks. A gift, no matter how wonderful, isn't meant to be worshipped above its Giver. Let's reclaim the biblical calling we have to share with others, connect through food, and serve one another as Jesus did.

Let go of the fear and unrealistic expectations. Have that dinner party. Cook for your family. For a starter cook, dinner can be chicken breasts marinated in some lemon juice, olive oil, and a little garlic and herbs. Then toss it on the grill or bake it at 350 degrees until done (about a half hour). See? You even have a recipe to make it happen. Grab your mismatched place settings, text a neighbor, and share life over food.

RSVP to the Invitation into Humility

- Proverbs 15:17 reminds us that food doesn't have to be fancy: "Better a small serving of vegetables with love than a fattened calf with hatred." Host a three-dish dinner party, which is exactly what it sounds like. Serve only three dishes. This will keep the focus on the people, not the presentation. Try a pot of chili, a garden salad, and cornbread. Or lasagna, a Caesar salad, and crusty Italian garlic bread. And notice how your simpler meal and lowered stress level affect your ability to connect with your guests.
- We always had our daughters take turns "presenting" dinner at the family table. Whoever's turn it was would explain what we were having, naming the basic ingredients, and then helping to plate everything. Having the children help with the plating not only demystified ingredients for them but also broke me of my own tendencies to focus on pretty plating. Now I instead find joy in my daughter serving me a meal. If you have any children in the house, have them help present and serve the food at dinner. Even

little kiddos can be in charge of tossing and scooping out salad. Bringing kids into the meal helps keep everyone focused on the joy of the food, not how fancy it is.

- Even the greatest chefs usually have a deep love of humble food. Next time you're in a restaurant that serves mostly artistic food, ask the server if there are any off-menu, simple home-food offerings available. Maybe there won't be, but often the chef will love to make something from his or her childhood. Having an awesome grilled cheese sandwich prepared by a talented chef is not only special but also a reminder that even artistic food is, at its core, God's food.

Chapter 11

The Premium Price of Processed Food

An Invitation into Work

The modern food system separates us from God, and the price is higher than we think.

I feel like I've been working my whole life! I've been a single career woman, a stay-at-home mom, and a mom who works out of the house. By the time I was thirty-six, I'd spent twelve years building a successful finance career in corporate America. I'd married an amazing man, had been sober for a number of years, and thought I had a pretty healthy sense of self and purpose. Looking back, though, I realize a large part of my identity was derived from success in my career. I'd invested a good deal of time in it, of course, and spent the majority of my days squeezing the maximum productivity out of each one. Then life surprised me big time. I had four beautiful kiddos in just two-point-five years (tip: contrary to popular myth, it is definitely possible to get pregnant while breastfeeding). I found myself pushed into totally unfamiliar territory. I became a stay-at-home mom, or SAHM, as we called ourselves.

For me, the hardest part about being a SAHM was the lack of reasonable and reliable feedback about my efforts. In the corporate world, if I worked extra hard on a presentation for the board of directors, that presentation was usually lauded as a success, resulting in short-term feedback such as kind words from the CFO and in long-term rewards such as promotions or career opportunities.

The work-reward loop in the world of a SAHM is so much less predictable. It feels random and unfair. The days when I feel particularly organized—with the diaper bag prepacked with everything from wipes to changes of clothing for the babies, bottles washed and prepped, snacks divvied up into small containers in anticipation of Mommy-and-me gym time—could unravel into complete disaster because of a totally unforeseen mishap. Maybe one or two (or four) of the kiddos had a meltdown or a last-minute diaper blowout, or someone barfed on my last clean shirt. The upside of this randomness is that some of the most magical Mommy moments would surprise me on days when I totally wasn't on my game, when the house was a mess, and when I didn't make it to Costco *yet again* to load up on diapers and groceries. Switching to this world where I was no longer even a tiny bit in control of what kind of day I would have was humbling and hard. Dependence on God can be a tough lesson to learn.

Another unfamiliar aspect of my new role as Mom-to-many was the need to make a real family dinner every night. Sure, I'd cooked my entire single and newlywed life, but getting dinner on the table for a full family took it to the next level. It also put me into an entirely new target market: I was the core demographic for the every consumer-goods company out there. Moms out there will agree: have kids, and you're immediately on the mailing list for every convenience item and processed food product in existence. Even the recipes I was exposed to as a new reader of parenting and ladies' home magazines relied heavily on processed food. I had no idea how many different ways a packet of onion-soup mix could be used in a slow cooker until I had babies! In my new life, recipes that involved layering in a bunch of processed foods together "in minutes" bombarded me, even in the recipes shared among the neighborhood moms, my new peer group. And through my moms groups, I learned about kids-eat-free nights at local fast-food joints. For me and most of my mom peers, *free* was a word that had taken on unprecedented appeal.

Switching quickly from dual-incomes-no-kids (DINKs) to single-income-four-kids inspired me to start clipping coupons, which subtly began to reinforce for me this concept of save-time-don't-cook. Why? Because coupons are abundantly available—and even doubled—for premade dressings and flavored noodles and frozen entrees. But just try to find a coupon for a head of lettuce or a pound of apples. You'll likely come up dry. Bargain shopping at the grocery store has a bias toward the interior aisles where the processed food is because that's where the coupon action happens.

I remember once scoring a coupon for gravy mix that, doubled, would make the product free. This felt like a no-brainer. I'd never made gravy from a mix before, so I thought I'd try it. When I located the product in the store, I was blown away. Nearly half an aisle (!) was devoted to these ready-made packets that flavor everything from meat loaf to taco meat to fajitas to, yep, gravy. I stood wide eyed, wondering if these product geniuses had simply done the (actually-not-so-hard) work of gathering all the herbs and spices in the correct ratios for us moms too busy raising our kiddos to be bothered.

I've always been a fairly healthy eater, but even I was open to a shortcut if it made sense. The ingredients on the back of most of the packets told a different story: they were full of sodium, MSG, preservatives, and anti-caking compounds. As my kiddos circled my ankles and tugged on my pants, I wondered: *Is it really so hard to dump a little fresh salsa instead of a packet of chemicals into a pan of ground beef to use for our tacos?* But I bought the gravy packet. After all, it was free, and I do love a bargain.

All the ads, free recipes, coupons, and magazine articles had somehow convinced me to go for the quick and easy, and from what I can gather, they had also convinced my fellow parents. We could win at the mom game: simply open cans and envelopes and dump them into our slow cookers, freeing up time to browse Pinterest or peruse the aisles of Michaels for scrapbooking supplies for baby books.

So I bought packets and bottles and boxes of prepackaged stuff with my coupons to make recipes I read about on the back of said packages. Soon my pantry morphed into a bulging mini-mart of processed snacks and goodies. Prepared foods that used to be a backup plan for an extra busy day became a way of life. And I even felt pretty good about it all because, being on a tight budget, I found it gratifying to see a full cupboard.

Besides, my bunco group loved my weird buffalo chicken dip made 100 percent from chemical-laden packaged products dumped into a pan and baked. I had four kids under the age of three and a husband whose job had him out of town every single week Monday through Friday. So I certainly knew a thing or two about where to get the chicken nuggets shaped like Mickey Mouse (Costco) and which macaroni and cheese was the only one my toddlers wanted (classic Kraft in the blue box). I fueled up with cup after cup of whatever coffee was on sale—I'd add cinnamon to the grounds to hide any bitterness—and even drank Coke to keep the energy up. I was so tired that every day was a challenge to simply get through. My daily motivating goal was 7:00 p.m.—just get to 7:00 p.m., and all four will go to bed. In some ways, these really were not my best moments. In other ways, I look back at the circumstances and see a survivor. Depends on the day. Whether those moments were a digression into bad parenting or a rock-on-mama period of my life, I cannot deny that I felt awful. Eating tons of processed food takes an incredible toll on how we feel, both physically and emotionally.

Here is what I learned. First, gravy from a packet is disgusting, and just because something is cheap doesn't mean it's a bargain. But I learned a broader life lesson too. Shortcuts don't really exist for most things. Sure, there are best practices, but anything presented as a silver-bullet shortcut usually means you just haven't seen the downside yet. Oprah once said something that has stayed in my mind, and I think it's relevant here: if there were a single magic pill that could give someone the body of her dreams, she would take it. And if anyone could afford to have it, it would be Oprah. And if she doesn't have it, it's because this magic silver bullet doesn't exist. Shortcuts usually have a cost even if it's hidden, which is the case with a lot of processed food. Processed-food shortcuts may seem like a clever way to alleviate unnecessary work, but they leave out the high costs of eating that way.

Did you notice that phrase *unnecessary work*? Work gets a bad rap. Many of us want to avoid it, but have you ever lost yourself in your work, when time flew and you had absolutely no sense of what was going on around you? Work is wonderful! Using your gifts to create something of value through work feels like being close to God because we are doing what he intended for us to do from the moment he made us.

There is honor in work! God had Adam work in the garden, and we know work was considered good since God gave Adam tasks *before* he ate the forbidden fruit. Caring for God's creation and one another is holy work, but we are quick to try to escape every last bit of it when we can. That applies to our food and how we eat as well. Our modern food system is separating us from one another, from working to produce what we eat, and from God, and the cost is higher than we realize.

And that cost isn't just physical. When I bought into the idea that using processed food was better for me because it was easier for my schedule, my work and energy levels, I inadvertently removed myself from God's food system and his healthy, holy design for the way we should eat, and on my plate I saw only the handiwork of factories. It's nearly impossible to stay awed by the miracle of an onion growing when it's presented to you in dried brown bits in a packet of soup mix. By losing touch with what food really is—a gift—and what it costs to grow it, we set ourselves up as a society primed to make poor food choices about what we eat and how we are willing to grow it.

What We Really Pay

Imagine trying to manage your household budget, but when you shop at the grocery store, you can't see any prices. When we don't understand all of food's costs, our decisions are made in a vacuum, driven by our whims and best guesses.

What I was experiencing during that processed-food period was a microcosm of what had transpired over the last half century or so in America. When modern, industrialized, capitalist society showed up and offered to do the cooking for midcentury housewives, these housewives—underappreciated and weary—understandably jumped at the promise of reclaiming a sliver of time, just as I had.

Restaurants, takeout, and processed food proliferated like mushrooms. It wasn't just housewives who bought into this new system. For who can claim to have too much time? Whether parents, students, corporate-ladder climbers, entrepreneurs—we all feel like we don't have enough time. Even an extra half hour a day sounds pretty appealing. I know it did to me. And the corporate profits made sure that companies kept the offerings coming.

When I outsourced a big chunk of my cooking to snatch back a half hour a day, though, I failed to appreciate the full impact of that decision. The short-term gains do not outweigh the long-term costs, most of which are external—meaning costs that are passed along to an outside third party or society or our future selves to absorb—and not immediately evident.

This newfound half hour theoretically could give us more time to be together with our loved ones, but instead it's costing us connection with one another. When we shifted into buying more processed foods and takeout, we also shifted away from the table. Prepared and processed foods are easily consumable individually and increasingly away from the family dinner table: we eat alone, away from one another, or even in moving vehicles. "On-the-Go Eating" is an actual chapter title in a cookbook I once wrote (but never published), so I know that even those of us who make our living in food eat on the go. When we don't sit and eat with one another, we miss out on one of the reasons God made food so varied and delicious in the first place: so we could delight in it with others.

This disconnection extends beyond our relationships with one another, though. We also lose track of where our food is coming from, thus we're further separated from God's creation. Recently a friend's daughter found dirt in her salad at home and burst into tears. My friend reminded her that lettuce actually grows in the ground. Tears were dried, but the point was well made: the further we distance ourselves from creation, the easier it is to ignore the state of our planet, making it nearly impossible to steward it well. What we lose when we trade prepared foods for that freed-up half hour is the daily chance to both emulate our Creator and thank him for the raw materials he provides for our own creations.

We're also risking the health of our families and our own health. One of the most impactful decisions we can make about our health when it comes to food is who we allow to cook it. When I judge *Guy's Grocery Games,* I often remind contestants that buying processed food is like hiring a sous-chef you've never met and who probably doesn't cook the way you do. We have no idea what the makers of this processed food prioritize and what their value system is, but profit surely figures into the equation. We have no idea if they care about helping rather than harming creation, or if they just add some extra salt and color to make the food look and taste fresher and more nutritious than it is.

I mean none of this to judge or shame anyone. We don't need to feel guilty when our eyes are opened to a new truth. We don't even need to respond to that new truth with sweeping changes in our lifestyle. But it's worth giving some thought to the costs of processed food.

I spent nearly a year trying to reclaim a little extra time by buying processed food. But packets and lists of chemical ingredients and more than one over-salted meal made me crave the simplicity of whole foods I could recognize, even if they sometimes took a little more time to craft into a family-friendly dinner. When we switched back to mostly fresh, unprocessed foods—even though it meant more time and more work—that decision made all the difference in the world. Yes, in how we look—our outsides do reflect what's going on inside—but more importantly in how we feel, in our health, and in our connection with one another. Eating more whole foods takes a little extra time. There is no magic way to prioritize our health without spending a little bit of time on it. But the good news is that cooking a simple, fresh meal really takes less time than you might think. And I promise you, I received such great joy from knowing I was loving my body, my family's bodies, and the care of our earth and its creatures by creating meals God's way. That extra time I invested in cooking was well spent.

Balancing Time and Work

Of course, sometimes we really do want or even need the trade-off of convenience foods. When we have crazy days with work, kids' soccer practice and dance classes, commutes and homework, and we find ourselves with barely enough time to brush our teeth, a precooked meal can be a sanity saver. Single parents working multiple jobs might feel like they have no choice, and some people all across our great country live in food deserts where the closest they can get to a fresh salad is a can of spinach. Get that can of spinach and serve it with joy in your heart, sister, while we as a society work to change the system that dictates unfair access to fresh food. Sometimes circumstances mean we are eating processed food, and in our gratitude even for less-than-ideal meals, I believe firmly that God can bless our bodies then too. But we can't deny that what started out as a busy day's backup plan has morphed into a habit, and we are losing the will to cook at all, viewing it as a subpar way to spend a half hour and maybe even a waste of time. We started out relying on processed food to gain an extra half hour to play bridge with the neighbors and ended up raising generations who don't know how to cook enough simple meals to feed themselves.

So that's the loss column. But opting for processed or fast food is not all bad because we do gain precious time. And that's not a small thing! Some days we need that half hour just to get the car pool schedule to work. As a mom of four, I understand the stress of having a day scheduled down to the minute. "Not cooking" is the helper we call in occasionally. When *occasionally* becomes *frequently,* though, we need to rethink how to free up hours of spare time each week so we can get back to living according to God's food design for us.

So. What are we doing—really—with that newly free time?

I can answer for my family without any hesitation: we spend it in some form of screen time. I'm not proud to say it, but it's a 100 percent certainty that we spend at least a half hour a day on screens outside of work.

Do you spend a half hour on screens a day? The hard truth is, if you can find a half hour to play on screens, you have time to make dinner. Maybe you don't have to do it every night, but maybe a little more often than you actually pretend like you don't have time to do now?

Here is what we are doing now: instead of accepting God's invitation into intimacy with him through our food, we are going on Instagram. And that says to God: *My idea is better than yours.* There's nothing redemptive about scrolling through everyone's shiny social media feeds so that we can compare our bumpy blooper file to their sizzle reels. Instead, we could be creating a meal to nourish our family, honor the earth, and bring us closer to it.

And here's the real kicker: the marginal time difference between cooking our own food and buying it cooked is not as great as we think. Sure, it's possible to spend hours in the kitchen on a special meal, and days like that are actually some of my favorites. But on a given weeknight, we can easily get a simple dinner on the table in about thirty minutes. By relying on takeout or processed food, we get back that half hour, right? Wrong! We don't actually get that full half hour back. Even a drive-through, where the entire meal is cooked and packaged and presented to us ready to eat, will take ten or twelve minutes of our time. So we are talking about eighteen minutes, my friend! Are eighteen extra minutes really too much to spend in creative worship and communion with God in the kitchen? Sometimes, the answer is yes. But most of the time I want to consider the question more deeply: Is it worth the price we pay to get those few minutes back in our lives if we spend them on a nonspiritual, non-value-adding activity?

Note that not all processed food is equal: the less processed the food is, the closer to the food as it exists in nature, the better. Fresh beans and legumes are wonderful, but most of us don't have access to purchase them unless we have a truly well-stocked farmers market. Dried, shelled beans are a good backup option, preferable to canned beans, which are preferable to prepared canned bean soup. Staying up the food supply chain as far as reasonable is sometimes the best we can do.

Am I suggesting that everyone needs to be a cook to know God? Well, yes and no. The good news is that cooking need not be on the agenda for everyone every day. It makes far more sense to divide and conquer household tasks. I do most of the cooking, but my husband does other stuff, like taking out the trash and building the bookcases from Ikea. Still, everyone should know how to cook a few basic meals. No adult should be so disconnected from their food system that they don't know how to put together a simple meal or two. This is not the same thing as an adult not knowing how to put together an Ikea book-case! Sure, it's good advice to know how to assemble furniture, but God created food, not Ikea, in the book of Genesis. (And I know for sure he didn't create those weird little wrenches.)

Most of the time we have a problem not with an actual shortage of time but rather with our priorities. We simply would rather scroll through Facebook than bother making dinner from scratch.

There may not be a magic silver bullet here, but the solution isn't as overwhelming as you might think. A few simple meals in your reper-toire is all it takes. You can do this. Stock the pantry with some potatoes and hearty vegetables you can roast in a jiffy. Grab some frozen salmon fillets that you can pop onto a baking sheet. Save that pizza delivery for an actual pepperoni craving—because life without any pizza makes no sense, right?—not to carve out time for Instagram on a random Tues-day night.

Making convenience, preparation speed, and cost per calorie more important than God's purpose for food in our lives has invisible, exter-nal costs that we need to identify, name, and make more informed deci-sions around. Reframe the hassle of buying and preparing our meals and look at those tasks as the holy work of food that they are. The dollar-menu default at the drive-through is simply not a celebration of God's economy. We can do better, and I believe God wants us to.

RSVP to the Invitation into Work

- Open your cupboard and fridge. Consider the food sitting in your pantry right this minute. Is there a less-processed version of some of your ingredients that you could buy instead? For example, could you swap your packets of flavored instant oatmeal for whole oats you could boil up into oatmeal in minutes and simply add your own flavorings like fruit, cinnamon, or maple syrup?

- Find a few easy recipes you can make quickly with pantry ingredients, and stock your pantry with those items on your next trip to the grocery store. Memorize these recipes and lean on them the next time you have a hectic evening and need to get dinner on the table quickly. Consider this extra bit of effort as being dedicated to God: "Whatever you do, work at it with all your heart, as working for the Lord, not for human masters" (Colossians 3:23).

- Decide for yourself that you will not eat processed food on the go. Choose "processed" or "on the go," but not both for any one meal. If you order a pizza, commit to sitting at a table to eat it. If you have to eat a meal on the go, take the time in advance to make it as homemade as possible. Buy a thermal lunch bowl, and you'll be amazed how quickly you can fill it. In a pinch even cheesy scrambled eggs will do the trick.

Chapter 12

Taking Pleasure in God's Food

An Invitation into Delight

God made the world delicious for a reason.
We can trust his system and satisfy our
palates with his food.

God created us, and he created the food to feed us, as we can read about in Genesis. He created us to get hungry so we would eat, he created the perfect food to feed us, and he gave us taste buds to take pleasure in the food he created. It sounds like a perfect, easy recipe. Yet we pull ourselves from the lovely cycle God created and instead create our own whirlwind of food anguish, and it goes something like this:

In our human imperfection and gluttony (more is more!), we twist God's gift and use it in ways he never intended. In our abuse of the gift, we disrupt God's system and train our palates to eat in a way that God didn't intend. To satisfy that morphed, imperfect palate, we scarf down salt, fat, and sugar in quantities and concentrations that our bodies were never intended to consume. We get sick. And we feel guilty about our eating habits, which creates a whole culture of guilt-driven language and behaviors of punishment and reward. We realize our palates have become accustomed to eating these goodies to our detriment, but rather than step back and reevaluate the harm our new cycle is bringing us, we decide to trick the system and give the palate what it wants without the associated costs: enter the fake sweeteners, fake fats, and quick-fix crazy diet fads that make manufacturers literally billions of dollars a year. Billions of dollars a year to maintain this palate-food cycle, which is completely outside the system God created for us.

Then to make everything worse, we feel guilty because we know we aren't eating healthy foods, so we decide that we need to "earn" the right to eat by working out or that when we do eat, we should shame ourselves into going to the gym to work off the calories. (Ugh! Do not get me started on the language we use in media around the holidays to discuss food: "guilt-free" recipes? Receiving a gift from God should be free of guilt!) The concept of guilt in food makes no sense when you think about it. God isn't bummed out when we enjoy his food, so why are we?

Certainly, getting back to God's original plan—using the food he gave us from the earth he created, preparing it, and consuming it in the manner and quantity he intended—would result in his best for us— our best health, our best weight, our best emotional well-being. But getting out of the spin cycle of modern Western eating is much easier said than done. It begins with accepting the beautiful truth that God made food delicious on purpose, and we can delight in it, gratefully accepting the gift.

Accepting God's Good Gifts of Food

My daughter Charlotte starting baking with me before she could even walk, and by the age of nine, she could in earnest make her own legit cake recipes. Her specialty was dreamy orange mini-cupcakes that she would make for family birthdays, which included her three sisters, her parents, and all five of her cousins who lived down the street, plus holiday celebrations with neighbors and friends. When I asked her why she had picked orange over more obvious options like chocolate and vanilla, she said that oranges are more complex and interesting, that their skins are like perfume with a touch of bitterness, and that inside they are both sweet and a little sour. An orange is like life, she said, which is a perfect way to celebrate a birthday.

Charlotte's orange cupcakes became legendary (I have permission to share her secret: a mix of lemon and orange juice, but shh!)—and rightfully so. She would spend hours on the project, making the perfect light batter for a buttery, tangy, and tender crumb. Her American buttercream required a known-only-to-Charlotte exact ratio of cream cheese to butter, so the icing held just a hint of sour without veering off into a carrot-cake frosting vibe. And Charlotte became a cupcake-decorating expert, a skill she acquired herself, mostly by watching YouTube videos. Even the tray to hold the cupcakes was always decorated, each birthday different from the last. The result was special, tailor made for the birthday girl (or boy). In fact, as I type this, Charlotte is holed up in the kitchen baking something top secret for her sister who just came back from several weeks away at a residential ballet program. Bakery-surprise-cookery really is her love language.

Delectable treats such as Charlotte's creamy cupcakes produce complex emotions, ranging from pleasure to guilt. Why is that? Should we feel shame when we enjoy certain foods? Remember that God made everything for us, including our food system, out of his generosity and love for us.

God made the world much yummier than he needed to. If God intended for food to be purely fuel, he would not have made peaches so tasty. He could have easily created a more efficient, less delicious, system of nourishment than what we have. In fact, he could have skipped the notion of taste altogether.

Instead, he gave us sweet plums and grassy asparagus and tangy olives and luscious figs and creamy avocados and silky-sweet honey. He gave us sweet and salty and fatty things, each one with its unique function. He didn't give us these so we'd be tortured with all the deliciousness we shouldn't have, but to enable us to partake in the pleasures of eating his food! The problem enters the equation when we eat them in a way God did not intend, which could include giving too much power or praise to food itself instead of to our Creator God, or simply removing ourselves completely from his food cycle and creating our own food system with its set of tricks, like eating sweet things that don't have calories or following extreme rules like eating only a block of cream cheese a day to lose weight (yes, this is a thing!).

The Bible holds many clues that tell us God loves a good meal. In Genesis we read that one of the first things God did for humanity was set up the food system. In Exodus, when God fed the Israelites with free bread that fell from the sky (manna), he made it taste sweet like honey. Throughout the Gospels we see that Jesus spent much of his ministry eating, and many times when he shared the gospel or performed a miracle, Jesus was either eating, sharing a meal, going to a meal, or coming from one. And in Revelation when Scripture talks about God's final kingdom, it's depicted as a huge feast. While there are limitations we are to follow in receiving all of God's gifts, God seems pretty happy about the food he has given us.

Food is indeed a gift from God, and we can delight in it with gratitude and joy. The culture of guilt around food pleasure—"being good" about what we are eating, earning dessert by eating healthy first, or working off a special treat—is man's idea, not God's, and I think it may be rooted in the deep knowledge that we have slowly moved away from the food cycle God created for Adam and the rest of humanity. The guilt comes from our human tampering with God's system and using food in ways he did not intend.

No Substitutions, Please

When we quietly know we are operating outside of God's best system for us, our knee-jerk reaction isn't to step back and get closer to nature and God's food system. It's guilt—and then reactive panic. We move into a world of weird and unhelpful dieting that includes illogical conclusions like deciding not to eat tomatoes because they have too much sugar but then downing a bright blue, sugar-free "sports drink" that is loaded with fake sweeteners—but considered healthy because athletes drink it.

God gave us deliciousness because he loves us and wants to invite us into delight. When we reject the food we see in nature, we reject his gift, pure and simple.

I wonder how it makes him feel when we reject nature—his food—in favor of chemical-laden food-like substances. Artificial flavors, preservatives, colors, and sweeteners are human attempts to trick the system, meaning we want to taste something sweet like sugar, but we don't want the consequences—usually the calories—associated with sugar. So we drink a diet soda, but then avoid fresh tomatoes in name of "health."

My daughter Margaux once read a fruit-candy label that said "artificial strawberry flavor," and she asked earnestly why anyone would use fake strawberries when we have them already in nature. She decided that they must have been out of season and perhaps the producers wanted to make this candy in winter. There's wisdom in Margaux's confusion! Why consume artificial flavors of things that actually exist? If we want to taste strawberries, let's eat a strawberry. If not, make up your own flavors, people. Strawberry is already taken.

I say all of this not because I have it all figured out and have conquered the beast of our confusing relationships with food. I have a definite sweet tooth. I've always been wary of artificial sweeteners. Logically, I figured that if I was worried about how much sugar was in, say, my soda, then perhaps I was just drinking too much soda. The answer, it seemed, was to consume less soda rather than swap it out for a calorie-free version.

Even with my relentless pursuit of healthy, godly eating, I found myself far outside of God's ideal food system, and I didn't even feel myself slip away. I don't know if it was the glossy commercials or social acceptance or pressure or the fact that these calorie-free sweeteners suddenly showed up from "natural" sources, which completely removed the word *artificial* from the equation. But somewhere along my path, I started drinking diet soda. In fact, I actually preferred Diet Coke (the real Coke was "too sweet"!). Once I was on the diet-soda bandwagon, other "diet" foods seemed like a reasonable way to cut calories. Pancake syrup that was practically calorie-free? Yes, please!

We want to outsmart God's design. How can we get concentrated levels of sweetness without the consequences? But the real issue is that maybe God doesn't want us to eat concentrated levels of sweetness. Think how hard it would be to find anything in the natural world that has as many grams of sugar, with as few other nutrients or benefits, as one soda. Even a huge piece of fruit would likely not have as much sugar. And a piece of sugary fruit also contains helpful things: fiber, vitamins, and other nutrients that keep the sweetness from being absorbed too quickly. It'd be difficult to consume an entire pineapple, for instance, since the fiber would fill you up so much. God cleverly designed fruit to have reasonable consummation limits. But it's become totally acceptable to drink several sodas in one sitting, as evidenced by the continued popularity of Big Gulps across America. A Big Gulp has way more sugar than a pineapple and absolutely zero limiting factors or other nutrients to keep you from slurping your way to being jacked up on a sugar high.

God created our appetites, and he created the food to satisfy those appetites. We can trust his system of feeding us. We can celebrate the palate we've been given and stop tinkering with God's handiwork. Our palates today might crave the salt and fat and sweetness we've trained them to expect. But once we drop our modern habits and turn back to real food—food where we can see nature (God's fingerprints) on the plate—our palates will adjust. It really takes only a couple of weeks of eating the way our Maker intended—whole foods, prepared and eaten mindfully, shared with others—for our bodies to normalize its cravings and get us back into God's food-feedback loop where our given palates are satisfied by the food God gave us. Suddenly, a simple peach plucked from the tree tastes gloriously sweet, exactly how our Creator designed it.

Believe Wholly in What You Eat

It makes complete sense that my work helped me clarify my personal stance on artificial sweeteners, flavors, and colors—but it wasn't easy. Working in food makes gaining and maintaining a healthy perspective more challenging since a job in food media often involves partnering with various products. I'm sure you've seen this happen in your social media feeds: a food company pays a celebrity, or "influencer," to create recipes with its product, and then share that recipe with their audiences, who then go out and buy that company's product. Simple marketing. In a perfect world, the talent is sharing a product they actually feel great about and truly believe will improve the lives of their audience, the fans get to learn more about a product in a way that is less annoying than sitting through TV commercials, and the company enjoys access to a new audience. An added bonus is that these endorsement deals usually pay the talent's mortgage so they can create more recipes and put them on the internet for free. These kinds of arrangements, if done right, can be a win all around.

Again, ideally, the talent really loves the product and might be telling you about it anyway. Sometimes a brand notices an influencer talking about their product, so they reach out to turn the relationship into something more official. But introducing money into the food-recommendation equation can be tricky. There can be some big numbers behind some of these deals, which means there's a slippery slope that can end in the talent talking about a product they don't believe in at all.

Early in my career, I once came so close to signing with a company to promote a product I liked well enough, but I had some tiny reservations about. I knew I wouldn't necessarily buy this product consistently for my family, but I was new to the business and lacked the confidence and wisdom to listen to my gut. I justified it by reasoning "that's just how these things work." I felt an uneasiness during the whole negotiation period as I managed to convince myself I could make the talking points work. When the deal randomly fell apart, I was actually more relieved than disappointed. I resolved never to make a deal like that. If that's how the business works, that small part of the business will have to go on without me.

Feeling confident about the food I eat is important, and I believe it is just as important to support fully the food I recommend to others. So I started to ask myself these questions before signing up for endorsements: *Do I have the product in my house right now? Do I have a story about that product? Would I ever tell a friend or my kids about this product?*

A few years ago, my agent, Jeff, called with an offer from a no-calorie ("all-natural") sweetener. Theoretically, it checked out: I had that product in my home in various forms, such as low-calorie pancake syrup and protein powder. I actually started to snap my photos and craft my stories to email Jeff back—my way of letting him know that I love the product. But I hesitated. Something small stirred in me, and it caused to me to stop and consider if I truly wanted other people buying this sweetener, a product intended to give us concentrated levels of sweetness for fewer calories. I had this unsettled feeling that this product was outside of God's best for anyone who was listening to my voice for food wisdom. Would I want my own children to purchase this product? The answer was no. (Fellow mama, isn't it funny that we see in our behavior how little we value ourselves only when we realize we would never wish that behavior upon our children?) If I wouldn't tell my fans and my kids to buy this product, it had no business being on my own shelves! I declined the offer, but more than that: I threw away everything in my pantry that had fake sugar, flavors, or color in it. The flip side to this rejection of the fake is the joyous, pure, wonderful experience of loving the food God did give us. No apology or guilt. Just delight!

That's not to say I'll never drink a diet soda again. I try not to be too dogmatic about anything, even health. But I fiercely believe that artificial anything isn't part of God's best for us. If we are using an artificial something regularly, it may be worth considering whether we're trusting God's food to satisfy our palates and if our palates may have been altered by the behavior resulting from this lack of trust.

Food Checks and Balances

God created an extraordinarily complex world with checks and balances and intricacies that amaze me. In his perfect system, we are given plants, vegetables, and fruit for food. (Later, in Genesis 9, he added meat.) God, who knows the number of hairs on my head, is definitely wise enough to create the food that will best nourish my body and keep it healthy. Wouldn't it make sense for God to provide satisfaction for the sweet tooth I seem to have? He does provide for my human desire to have salty, sweet, and fatty flavors in a plethora of natural foods in quantities and ratios that are healthy for my body. When I decide my palate needs more sweetness than I know is right for my body and I turn to artificial sweeteners, I realize I am not valuing God's equilibrium. I am saying to him that I don't trust his ability to satisfy my tastes with the food he has given; I'm saying that I am smarter than he is.

God created me and the food my body needs. I don't need people in a lab figuring out how to fake out my taste buds. When I see man's fingerprints on my food more than I see God's, I'm on a slippery slope of self-reliance that can easily seep into the rest of my life.

Accepting God's food system as being the perfect one to satisfy your palate is an acknowledgment of your dependence on him. Yes, there are limits. We aren't intended to eat all sugar and no protein. We really are created to eat a lot of plants and veggies. Don't like veggies yet? If you eat them anyway, your palate will adjust. (Really!) Besides, remember that eating veggies is receiving God's best gift for you. Receive his gift. Eat the peaches. Have an occasional cupcake when your daughter makes it for you. Enjoy God's delicious world.

RSVP to the Invitation into Delight

- Ask yourself a simple question before eating: Do I see God in the food I am about to eat? This will change the way you eat, I promise! By the way, if you are imagining a white-knuckle world of denying sugary treats and having a piece of fruit for dessert every day for the rest of your life, you'll be glad to know that palates adjust fairly quickly once you eat God's way—and one cupcake your daughter makes you won't derail everything.
- Pray for the willingness to trust that God was deliberate in how he chose to feed us: "God said, 'I give you every seed-bearing plant on the face of the whole earth and every tree that has fruit with seed in it. They will be yours for food'" (Genesis 1:29). In our culture, advertising and marketing are so pervasive

that we sometimes don't even notice its impact. To remind yourself to trust God more than a lab or an advertising firm, offer up this simple prayer often: "Help me, God, to trust your system of food and help restore my palate to one that is satiated by the nourishment you provide."

- Watch your language. We start to believe what we hear ourselves say—and so do our kids. When we talk about food being "bad" or we use the language of guilt about eating, we take steps away from God, who is hoping to use food to draw us closer. Instead of doling out a treadmill "punishment" for eating a slice of pie at a girlfriend's house, why not celebrate the connection you make while eating that pie? And then celebrate your body's ability to move by getting on the treadmill. They are both gifts: the pie and the treadmill. One isn't atoning for the other.

- Be kind to yourself and to others. Birthdays happen. Road trips happen. Don't get caught up stressing over the occasional sugar or fat bomb. The small things you do consistently matter so much more than the big thing you do rarely. If you eat clean food daily but scarf down a Big Mac once a year, your palate is not likely to change. So be kind to yourself and to others. Every meal is a new chance to draw closer to God.

Chapter 13

Loving Our Bodies as God's Masterpieces

An Invitation into Acceptance

The world wants us to love our bodies
by changing them, but Jesus wants us
to love ourselves unconditionally.

have a somewhat complicated history with food and my body. Perhaps
you can relate.

Not always having enough food shaped my initial views as a child.
I always felt the need to fill my plate completely anytime I could. Then,
as an adult, I took in the world's many mixed messages and found myself stuck in no-man's-land of wanting to eat healthy but somehow slipping into eating specific foods in order to get thinner—and my goal
was not to make my body its best temple for God, even though 1 Corinthians 3:16 tells us that our body is God's temple. There is a fine line
between eating healthy and exercising as a way of worshipping God and
caring for his temple *and* eating healthy and exercising in order to be

pretty or admired by the world. The behaviors look very similar. But they are different in a crucial way: one is worshipping the Creator, and the other is worshipping the world he created.

God created us in his image, and he loves us deeply. If I am receiving this love fully, my natural response would be one of tremendous gratitude for how he made me. The same God who created the beautiful mountains and oceans created our bodies. Yet if I am honest with myself, for much of my life I haven't been grateful for my body.

The best way I can describe my attitude toward my body was a grumpy acceptance of the subpar lot I had drawn. I've always joked about having "childbearing hips" long before I ever knew I'd have four girls, as well as my inability to have bangs because of my pudgy face and my tendency to gain a pound just by looking at a holiday pie. Harmless self-effacement, I thought. One of my dearest girlfriends, Karen, taught me something when she heard me make a self-deprecating remark. She said, "I don't like the way you are talking about my precious friend." She helped me realize it's unkind and ungrateful to speak ill of my body. Do you do this too?

All these tiny jabs are not directed at ourselves; they are actually directed at God. He tells us we are "fearfully and wonderfully made" (Psalm 139:14) and then we respond by saying, "Your handiwork is just not good enough for me."

What would happen if we were grateful for our bodies instead? What if we believed that we are complete in Christ? What if, when we look in the mirror, we saw ourselves through God's eyes and saw the beauty he sees? What if we all were magically transformed like Amy Schumer in *I Feel Pretty*? She hits her head at the gym and wakes up suddenly thinking she is beautiful, and because she believes in her own beauty, everyone else does too. What if we simply chose to see our beauty, trusting that God's eyes are more qualified than our eyes and society's eyes?

No More Listening to the Lies

If you ever visit my little town of Coronado, a small island off the south side of San Diego, you'll get there by way of the Coronado Bay Bridge. It's a majestic structure spanning two full miles. The view from up there—endless and gorgeous stretches of blue water dotted with boats—always fills me with awe. My entire body exhales at the sight.

The Coronado Bay Bridge is also one of the top suicide sites in America.

I like to run along a trail that takes me right under a slice of the bridge. The view underneath differs starkly from the view above. Water that looks fresh and inviting when seen from above seems dark and deep in the shadow of the giant concrete structure. The air temperature even drops beneath the bridge. It's eerie.

The first time I jogged there, the sight of just one of the enormous columns supporting the bridge stopped me in my tracks. The sheer massiveness of it made me feel so small. I stood still as cars roared by overhead and small splashes of water lapped below. A seagull's cry broke the rhythmic sounds of my heartbeat and jogger's breath. Then my gaze shifted from the huge column to the dark water, then to the vast space between the top of the bridge—so far above—and the water below.

It struck me then that this space between the bridge and the water had witnessed so much pain, so many regrets too late to reverse. I prayed for that space. I prayed that it would be filled with God's love and that, in those few critical seconds, desperate souls would find whatever grace they'd been missing. I prayed for the bridge up top, for the next person who climbed there, eager to leave the vortex of despair. I prayed about those who'd already jumped. I cried and prayed some more. I thought of my mom, who knew too well that moment of hopelessness before taking her own life. Then I walked home, too spent to run farther.

The next time I ran, I stopped again, prayed for a minute or two, and then kept running. I did it again the next time. Soon this turned into a regular practice, my own spiritual discipline. I prayed for those affected by suicide at the Coronado Bay Bridge; for those hovering at the top, debating whether to jump; for those we've lost; and for those struggling with depression or other mental conditions.

As I shared with others about this practice, followers on social media began to send me names of relatives and friends to pray for. I wrote their names on a piece of paper I folded and kept tucked into my shoelaces to pull out and read during my prayer break under the bridge. This was not a cheerful exercise, but it was worth practicing because I felt close to God there. He met me every time. It was good. The experience felt sacred as I prayed for others and spent time with God, time for him to shape my heart more fully into who he created me to be.

One day I simply didn't have time to stop. Or at least that's what I told myself. My husband and I were days away from our tenth anniversary. The plan was to renew our marriage vows in a ceremony we'd share with family and friends. We hoped to refresh our deep commitment to each other and our four daughters. The *Huffington Post Weddings* had asked for exclusive coverage of the event. I wanted to lose an extra pound or two before photos of me in a flowy halter dress blasted out for all the world to see.

So instead of stopping to pray under the bridge, I ran past my normal spot, thinking that just this week, the priority was getting slim. I'd also skipped my morning devotional for a few days, too busy planning an event and a meal that would impress. God would understand, right?

I kept running. Another half mile into that run, it hit me: *I was choosing skinny over God.* I was preparing my body for photographs to be judged by the world's standards when what mattered—if I looked deeply enough—was preparing my heart for my recommitment to my husband and our family. I wasn't running to honor God and the body he gave me. I was running to look good enough for strangers and to achieve their confirmation of my worth. And what was worthy according to the world? Being thin.

Realizing I'd chosen trying to be skinny over spending time with God was a huge wake-up call for me. I made a decision—I put myself on a workout-and-diet fast. I reallocated my daily workout time to devotional time, preparing my heart for the vow renewal.

It wasn't easy. Shame quickly rushed in. *Quit eating and get back out there and run so tomorrow you can be prettier than you are today,* whispered a voice in my head. *Keep your eye on the (skinny, pretty) prize. Nothing tastes as good as skinny feels.*

All lies. And the worst kind of lies—half truths! The liar was using a label I'd been given as a young girl, when they called me "the smart one" and my sister, Stacy, "the pretty one." That harmless social shorthand intended to distinguish two little blondes stuck with me my whole life and mocked me.

I could almost feel the flesh under my arms getting softer and more pillowy. Maybe the smart thing to do *was* to get back to diet and exercise. My husband would love me no matter what, but if he had a choice, he'd surely pick me more beautiful than ugly, right?

Skinny, slender, thin—all mere adjectives, innocent descriptors, but they have morphed into a synonym for beauty. We have Satan to thank for that. Satan works his best evil in half truths. Why? Because outright lies are too obvious, and people are often too smart to get caught up in an outrageous lie. Not always, but usually. We all pretty much know not to answer those emails written by an imprisoned prince in Nigeria—they are just too obviously fake. But a cleverly worded email seemingly written from a major company like Microsoft saying your account has been hacked and you need to sign in again to protect it—you might fall for it if the email address contains some elements of truth.

Satan is less like the Nigerian-prince email and more like the big-company trick. Scripture refers to Satan as a schemer and deceiver. Instead of writing ridiculous emails from Africa, he writes clever ones from email addresses that sound legit. By taking a tiny nugget of truth and wrapping it up in a big fat lie, he works his way into our minds and hearts. We cling to the tiny particle of truth as we swallow the whole ugly package. So Satan probably just loves that words like *skinny, slender,* and *thin* have become our social shorthand for *beautiful.* He has been doing this kind of twisting for a long time. Over and over we witness this in the Bible: it's usually a bit of truth that he distorts. We see the serpent speaking in half truths to Adam and Eve and erroneously quoting Scripture to tempt Jesus. In both cases Satan twisted God's words.

When I told myself I was trying to be healthy and fit and vibrant for myself and my family, I was only being half-honest. I wanted to be healthy and fit—admirable goals—but the deep-down truth was I really wanted to be fit to be pretty and admired by the world—and to feel good about myself, whose aesthetic has been shaped by the world. The nugget of truth here is that we are created to eat healthy, to move our bodies, to eat with a level of discipline, and to avoid gluttony. But Satan regularly adds to the notion of eating healthy food and exercising and turns it into a huge lie that society has bought into: the thinner, the better. Think about that for a minute. Is that a lie you believe too?

Navigating this slippery slope lined with half truths is tricky business. There is a fine line between eating healthy in worship of God and eating healthy because I want to be pretty or admired. Without daily, vigorous prayer, I cannot be counted on to know the difference.

This path paved with half truths is why so many of us, particularly women, have such a hard time balancing diet, health, and body issues in a healthy way. If we were certain our motives were pure, we'd pray to God, hand our food selections over to him, and let his strength fill the gap where our willpower falls short. But we don't do that. And it's not because the idea hasn't occurred to us. At our very core we know we're not always seeking fitness because we truly want God's will for our bodies. We seek fitness because we're seeking skinny, striving to meet a societal definition of bodily perfection, and we simply can't live with the incongruence of praying for that.

On the flip side of this equation is my own sloth, also a sin. Left to my own devices, I'd sleep in every day, never break a sweat, and lounge around in stretchy pants eating take-out Thai curry. Not pretty, I realize. And certainly not what God has in mind as my best me. His best for us includes healthy quantities of movement and food that fuel our bodies and keep them strong. God's best also includes trusting his vision for us and loving ourselves, including our bodies, unconditionally.

Time for a Heart Change

For me, staying in shape and feeling my best take effort because I've always tended toward gaining weight. Even events rumored to "melt away the pounds," like the stress of planning a wedding or the energy it takes to breastfeed, do nothing to slim me down. I worked out for hours in the gym for each ounce of weight I lost before my wedding day. Breastfeeding four babies in two and a half years resulted in almost no weight loss until I dieted and exercised. I've been on every diet known to humankind, including extreme diets that featured mostly eating one food like dry popcorn or fresh grapefruit. I've turned down God's gorgeous carrots because they had too much sugar and then guzzled a diet drink laden with gross chemicals, all in the name of fitness. And there was the regrettable weight-shedding cabbage soup diet incident that gave me horrible breath and irritability in exchange for lean thighs. So I don't throw out this accept-yourself-without-crazy-dieting-to-get-thin notion casually.

Even given a healthy diet and exercise, deviations in my routine quickly result in weight gain for me. Stress and shame ensue. I've felt my heart sink at the sight of too-thick arms in a photo, and I have cringed when I've felt an extra inch or two of my tummy fold over on itself. I've avoided swimsuit shopping in the spring, donning last year's instead and tucking myself into the poolside lounge chair, covered up by a sundress. Why couldn't I be like my husband, who notices matter-of-factly an extra pound or two that he may gain, but it sure doesn't let it stop him from jumping around the pool with our daughters? Why did my body stress me out so?

You might know this pain too. So many of us, particularly women, suffer with body image and esteem issues related to diet and exercise. Every year we are inundated with a slew of "New Year, New You" books—most with a white-knuckle, mean-and-lean approach to self-care. They address our lack of love for our bodies by suggesting we fix those bodies. The underlying message is that women will love their bodies by *making them lovable. What if, instead of changing our bodies, we changed our hearts?*

Back to my bridge runs. When I realized I'd neglected my divine appointment in pursuit of an unattainable goal of looking perfect for the camera, I knew something had to give, something that would have implications far beyond my vow-renewal photo shoot. The Coronado Bridge incident was the start of my journey of laying food, exercise, and body-image issues squarely at God's feet. I invited him into the dark corners of my heart, a room I'd kept closed to him for years.

I thought that, with concentrated effort, I'd be able to get back on track and reconcile my faith with my body image. And I thought it would be quick. A one-and-done thing. I was wrong on both counts.

Food and body image are intimately connected, so I started at the beginning. Literally.

God made our bodies exactly the way he intended. Scripture tells us he called them "very good." The decision to make us in various shapes, sizes, and colors wasn't arbitrary or because he was clumsy with the mold. He wasn't like my toddler daughters making misshapen, lopsided meatballs with tiny tentative hands, lacking the expertise to make photo-perfect smooth, uniform meatballs. No. God's expert fingers executed his vision perfectly. His meatballs are exactly the shape he intended, so if I'm a lopsided meatball, well, then it's a beautiful choice made by my Maker.

When I declare that I hate my thighs or refuse to get in a photo with my kiddos because I'm feeling ugly, I'm essentially thumbing my nose at God's artisanship. When my words and prayers say I trust God and his plan for my life, but on a practical level I deny the goodness of his handiwork, I'm placing more value on what society says is pretty than on what God says. Disdain for my body means I'm trusting the world's definition of beauty more than God's. Pure and simple.

Scripture also showed me that our bodies are designed to be fed with God's food and to move and be physically active. God wants us to take care of our bodies and honor him by eating nourishing food and exercising. Leaning into who we are meant to be is in itself worship. And it's worship because we're saying, *I honor you, God. I trust you.*

Eating well and exercising are my way of showing up for life as my full, best self. With all that God has given me, that's the best and most grateful response. In Philippians, Paul wrote: "Do not be anxious about anything, but in every situation, by prayer and petition, with thanksgiving, present your requests to God. And the peace of God, which transcends all understanding, will guard your hearts and your minds in Christ Jesus" (4:6–7).

I've read this verse many times before, but it took me years to catch this: "Do not be anxious about *anything*"? Really? Could Paul actually mean it? Writing from prison, Paul had so much more than a little belly fat to worry about. *The Message* version puts it this way: "Don't fret or worry. Instead of worrying, pray. . . . It's wonderful what happens when Christ *displaces worry* at the center of your life" (emphasis mine).

What a grand and glorious promise! Could it be that I was allowing the stress over my body to edge out Christ? And when I prayed under the bridge, was I putting my requests before my gratitude? I decided to switch it up and see what difference it would make.

My prayers and preparations—not just for my vow renewal—took on a new flavor after that. Leading with gratitude came pretty easily. Just looking back on the ten years Philippe and I had spent together brought lots of joy, and looking ahead made me feel similarly happy.

The vow renewal took place on the beach and included all four of our girls, and each had a chance to share what she treasured about our family. We all took a small scoop of sand and poured it into a conch shell to represent our individuality that was now forever mixed together as a family. How could I feel anything other than thankful? Exactly as the verse said, love and gratitude displaced any shame, fear, or worry. True peace descended.

I've since resumed my runs and I always stop at the bridge, but now I make gratitude the start of my prayer. I receive the gifts God has given with thanks before I make a single request. Sometimes my gratitude is so intense that I realize I have all I need.

I still exercise, and I continue to eat mostly healthy foods. So perhaps on the surface someone might not notice a difference in my shift toward Christ-centered fitness. But I know for me there's a huge difference between my exercising as a form of praise to God for the gifts he has given me and my exercising as "punishment" for taking the kids out for an ice cream cone.

I'm discovering a love and gratitude for my body that were not contingent upon my being a certain size or shape. Getting into shape and *then* loving my body was how I had done it in the past. There is such freedom in finding gratitude for what we have, whatever that is, whatever our body is like today. And verbalizing gratitude to God for our body each day helps! Literally thanking God for my legs helped me not cringe over dimples in my thighs. This may sound like a silly *Saturday Night Live* Stuart Smalley exercise, but this habit has done incredible things for my sense of self and my body image, and I continue to do this even today.

That's not to say I've totally defeated my tendency to grumble and complain about my body. I turned fifty this year, and the challenge is real! But the answer for me lies in daily connection to God through my morning devotions and prayer, because the reprieve I get from the ugliness of self-loathing needs to be refreshed every day. I can still find myself sometimes slipping into old thought patterns, but then I rely on the verse that started this journey for me. I remember to replace worry with Christ at the center, and I pray.

Acceptance of who you are, right in this very moment, isn't the endgame, and acceptance is not defeat. Acceptance is finding God's grace right where you are, exactly how you are, today. It's a loving starting point filled with gratitude, and it's acknowledging that you *are* worthy and lovable exactly how you are simply because that's how God created you.

RSVP to the Invitation into Acceptance

Here are some suggestions that have helped me keep my motivation pure in this complicated, messy place of diet, exercise, health, and bikini dreams:

- Offer a quick prayer of thanksgiving before eating anything and before hitting the gym. It will slow you down and help you focus on what matters: God. Does praying before exercise seem weird? Maybe. But it's magical. Asking God to help you keep your exercise worship focused on him, not the glossy magazine covers, is powerful!

- Ask God to guide you in both what you eat and the context. Pray, "God, how do you feel about me eating *x* in *y* context?" The context is important because not all foods are meant to be eaten all the time, but they might make sense in certain contexts. For instance, "God, how do you feel about me eating an ice cream cone with my kids at the park on Sunday afternoon?" is probably going to yield a different answer than "God, how do you feel about me eating a big bowl of ice cream every night while binge-watching *The Real Housewives*?"

- Hating our bodies is trusting the worldly definition of beauty more than God's definition. In Romans 12:1–2, Paul reminded us to "offer your bodies as a living sacrifice, holy and pleasing to God—this is your true and proper worship. Do not conform to the pattern of this world, but be transformed by the renewing of your mind." Add body gratitude to your morning prayer time. You might be surprised by the impact of this practice.

Chapter 14

Appreciating the Harvest

An Invitation into Dependence

In the garden, we are the planters and waterers. God is the one who transforms the seed.

God is the original gardener, and when he created Adam and Eve in his image, he made them gardeners too. The fruits of their labor would be their food: "The LORD God had planted a garden in the east, in Eden; and there he put the man he had formed. The LORD God made all kinds of trees grow out of the ground—trees that were pleasing to the eye and good for food" (Genesis 2:8–9). This isn't to say we are all called to be farmers—we all contribute to this complicated world in rich and different ways—but returning to the basic act of growing food, even just a little, will completely change how we view food. Seeing fruit on trees and vegetables growing in or on top of the ground is very different from seeing that same kind of produce sit there, all pretty and colorful, in neat piles at the grocery store. The act of gardening can also humble us by reminding us of our dependence on God, of how much we rely on his transformative hand to do the actual work of turning seeds into food.

I've always loved the smell of a farm—that familiar scent of cut grass, manure, and maybe a tinge of something sweet and fruity. The smell signifies home to me—odd since, growing up, my exposure to farms was mostly from the back seat of our banana-yellow station wagon when we headed out of town. But I did grow up sort of vacationing in farm country. I don't mean visiting one of those trendy work-farm situations where guests can volunteer to help out with farm chores like bottle-feeding cute baby goats before sitting down to a lavish country breakfast buffet of buttery biscuits, homemade sausage, and freshly laid eggs fried sunny-side up. I mean, we visited rural America in search of the cheapest lodging we could find. Even though we were broke, my mom firmly believed in taking a family vacation. We would fill up our Styrofoam cooler with a few days' worth of food—mostly hard-boiled eggs and the annual indulgence of "Chicken in a Biskit" crackers and cheese that squirted out of a can. We'd head out on vacation "to explore," which was code for *"We don't have the cash to go anywhere that requires an entrance fee like a Disneyland or a zoo."* She'd drive us on long stretches of two-lane highways, and we'd stay in roadside motels. The cheapest (family-friendly) motels were in rural spots where tourists are unlikely to stop to, say, squish their feet in warm cow poo, a favorite activity of ours. We kids didn't mind! A highlight of one trip was when our weary mom picked a roadside motel that advertised massaging beds on the billboard. We were only too happy to pay extra for this unheard-of luxury, begging Mom all night for more quarters to slip in the slot to make our beds hum and vibrate. We loved it and relished the unusual indulgence, but I don't think Mom slept much.

On those trips Mom would tell us stories about her childhood on the farm. Ancient history, so far as we could tell. Even though she'd left behind her dark, abusive home at the age of seventeen to move to Arizona, her childhood memories of time spent with cows and chickens and goats always brought a smile to her face.

Mom's affection for farm life took root in me perhaps because it was the only thing about her past that brought her joy. Though I still have never lived on a farm (although I secretly dream of it), I decided as an adult to get my fingers into the soil by planting a garden. Living in Paris, I started simple: growing a pretty extensive variety of herbs in window boxes I kept inside during winter and outside during the short Parisian summers. Growing herbs was hardly true farm work, but at least I was touching soil and witnessing the miracle of plants sprouting up.

Even this small agricultural gesture changed how I viewed food and how it tasted when I cooked it. I'd clip whatever herbs needed trimming and rub them into chicken skin with fatty European sweet butter, then roast the whole thing on top of new potatoes. The result was easily the best chicken I've had to this day. Even boring scrambled eggs came alive as a whole new creamy dish just by adding a small tweak of fresh herbs.

The positive impact of getting my hands dirty wasn't limited to my decidedly unsophisticated culinary experience. I discovered years later that even the world's best chefs revere soil! I once shared a fantastic dinner with Alex Guarnaschelli at a trendy farm-to-table restaurant in New York where she raved about a turnip, saying she could actually imagine what the soil tasted like that produced it. I was a little impressed—no one has a palate as discerning as Alex!—and a little stumped. Tasting the nuances of dirt seemed odd. And impossible. But Alex's words sank in, and over the years I've had this notion in the back of my mind. I'd always washed dirt off my produce as if it were an unwelcome intruder. But soil and vegetables are not enemies; they are partners in the same beautiful dance that produces energy and life in each of us. Taking time to eat slowly, actually striving to taste the earth that God gave us, makes sense, so why wouldn't we want to connect with the flavors of God's handiwork? Each slow bite of food we take can transport us into a place of gratitude and dependence on God.

Recently my daughter Valentine and I were traveling through Lancaster County, Pennsylvania, and a wonderful Amish woman named Sadie hosted us for a meal in her home. Immediately upon driving into farm country, as the familiar aromas of farm life made their way into the car, I felt my entire body relax. Dinner was so simple in both preparation and presentation that when we first sat at the table, I mentally calculated how many miles away the nearest restaurant was because we would certainly need a second meal to satisfy our modern Western appetites. A silent glance at Valentine confirmed that she agreed.

The entire meal centered on some unimpressive steamed baby potatoes in browned butter and shredded beets Sadie said she cooked for just a few minutes in an inch of salted water with a knob of butter. There was a small bowl of ham cubes, some homemade pickles, and a ramekin filled with a jiggly blob of ruby-red raspberry jam that Sadie had just made that afternoon, which we slathered on the gluten-free bread I carry for Valentine in my purse. Sadie asked me to say grace, and as I held the eighty-two-year-old widow's hand, lightly leathery from years of farm work, connecting in a circle with our fellow diners around the table, I would swear that even my heart rate slowed to match her Amish pace. Being nearer to God's soil can do that.

We ate slowly and relished our meal made of simple ingredients that, just hours earlier, had been deep in the ground of Sadie's garden, which produced nearly everything she needed to feed her family. The beets were so young she'd grated them with their skin on, and the tiny potatoes were just minutes old before they were cooked. Valentine and I tasted the earth, and it was glorious, and it made me question how *dirt* ever gained a negative connotation. This was pure, spectacular soil we were tasting—a tiny biome in itself, given by God and managed by Sadie. We ate mindfully, lingering over each incredible bite, as we were entertained by Sadie's many family stories—and, later, her harmonica playing, which turned into an impromptu sing-along. Somewhere in the joy of our new friendship and in the sharing of her garden's gifts, we found ourselves completely full, both body and soul. God, the original gardener, had provided abundantly, and we were humbled by his generosity.

Tasting the Soil Grows Our Gratitude

Gardening is harder than it looks and requires a willingness to relinquish control to various forces of nature. There can also be a back-and-forth, ongoing conversation between the grower and God. A gardener is constantly responding to soil conditions, weather changes, and the presence of insects or other living organisms, and the result is something like an overarching prayer at a macro level. Growing food involves far more planning and work than low grocery-store prices lead us to believe. Gardening takes work on our part and dependence on God to transform the seed. It takes patience for us to wait for the transformation to happen and the willingness to depend on God to deliver the results he sees fit. It turns out that gardening is a lot like life.

My first real garden taught me all these lessons. When we bought our home in Coronado, I planted my standard herb garden but decided it was time to attempt actual food. I started with tomatoes and peppers, both recommended for the sun patterns of our backyard. My sweet peppers turned out to be jalapeños despite the seed packet label. (As it turns out, when we sow a seed, it looks nothing like the fruit God might make!) I love spicy food and found a few dishes to flavor up with the jalapeños, but the harvest offered scarcely more than an occasional condiment. Definitely a far cry from the hundreds of sweet peppers I'd planned to serve my family.

Still, I had tomatoes that surely we could eat as an actual dish—if only I could garden them into bulbous maturity. But my tomato plants had tiny bugs that chomped away at the leaves, and then crabgrass sprouted up, stifling the plants' growth. Once I finally had actual small tomatoes growing, they were munched on by rabbits that sneaked in through unseen holes in our fences. My girls thought this was sweet, saying, "Oh, the rabbits are sharing our tomatoes, Mommy!" as if the critters were invited guests at our table. But they had a point: the rabbits just wanted to eat the same delicious food we did.

I sprayed the plants with vinegar (thank you, internet) and pulled up the weeds, and somehow my garden eked out a few sad, lonely tomatoes. They were small, bumpy, and irregular with blemishes and imperfections, and they looked nothing like a pile of even the most lackluster tomatoes you'd see at the neighborhood grocery store. In order to beat the bunnies, I harvested them a bit early. They were still warm from the sun when I sliced them and served them for dinner, and they were even harder than I'd expected. A critic might not have thought them very tasty, but to us, they were oh so sweet. All of us were thrilled to be eating them as part of our salad. We were the planters and waterers and caregivers working in partnership with the Gardener.

My second attempt at planting a garden was in a whole different climate, so my West Coast gardening expertise was useless. I was starting from scratch. We moved to the East Coast (just for a yearlong family adventure!) and spent the year living outside Washington, DC, in a huge house with plenty of land. I consulted the internet and asked the cashier at the local nursery for advice on what might grow well around our temporary home. Armed with the results of this admittedly sparse research, I decided to plant cold-climate-friendly brussels sprouts, one of my all-time favorite vegetables. I turned the planting day into a family project so my kids would learn valuable truths about our food system—and I could enjoy the free manual labor. Win-win. We planted all day. (Full truth: it was my birthday, so they could not say no or claim to be too busy to help. A little parenting hack to share with you, if I may.)

Winter came and then thawed, and I inspected the plants for small buds that might turn into full sprouts. I mentally planned for a spring filled with roasted brussels and shaved brussels sprouts salads, my two favorite preparations of that much-loved-by-me vegetable. One sunny day, I noticed tiny flowers blooming on the tips of the plants.

Oh, how gorgeous, I thought. *Perhaps the tiny buds will somehow turn into baby sprouts.*

It seemed improbable, but I believe God is capable of big things. My girls clipped the flowers for hairdos, since there were literally thousands to spare. But after more weeks of waiting, I saw nothing that spoke of a potential salad. Only floral decor bobby-pinned into elaborate braided buns that the kids learned on YouTube. This lack of progress was enough to make me consult a real gardener—the internet. It informed me that brussels sprouts only sprout every other year; they flower in the off years.

If you're a gardener, you already saw this coming, as did my next-door neighbors, who were not at all surprised when I informed them of this development. But this information threw me. I felt cheated! I'd planted and watered, yet there would be exactly zero sprouts for our family?

My brussels flowers would have to be enough joy from these plants this year. All my weeding and care and incessant checking in would benefit whoever lived in this home the year after we moved out. I began caring for the plants with someone else in mind. I'll confess it took a day or two, but that change of focus yielded its own satisfaction and joy. I was connecting with the unknown future residents through this soil.

Not even a week after my brussels sprouts revelation, I came across a random stalk of asparagus in our yard. Wild asparagus—was that even a thing? I certainly hadn't planted it. I happened to talk to our landlord that day, and I asked about the wild asparagus. Turned out that his wife had planted that asparagus long ago, before they knew they would move, and since asparagus takes several years to get going, this was the first year someone could actually eat it. "Enjoy the harvest," he told me. *Harvest* felt like a big word to use for clipping down a single stalk with kitchen shears, but I did it and roasted that lone stalk on a large baking sheet. I cut the stalk into six stubby pieces and served it to my family with the same joy with which I'd sliced up those lackluster tomatoes in Coronado. Each of us savored the inch or two of asparagus allotted to our plates.

That asparagus patch continued to grow, the stalks growing at near-impossible speeds. A stalk I considered too small to cut in the morning could be ready for roasting by dinner. The harvest window for asparagus is small, and an extra day of growth could turn a tender stem woody. As a result, we never had more than three or four mismatched stalks at a time, so I'd supplement with store-bought asparagus for dinner. In the grocery store, I'd buy twenty or thirty stalks at a time, all the exact same thickness, length, and color, and bunched together with a little blue rubber band.

I used to complain about how expensive asparagus is. I now considered it a pure miracle that someone could do this for $3.99 a pound. We ate this asparagus miracle daily all season long—it's the one vegetable that every family member loves—but the favorite stalks were the ones that grew in our yard, because as Charlotte said, "We can taste the soil."

Getting Closer to the Miracle of Food

Gardening teaches us patience and dependence on God; it also keeps us close to his food miracles that happen every day. Before planting our garden (can we call a tomato patch that yielded us a few weeks' worth of salad toppings an actual "garden"?), I was casually indifferent to the produce sitting abundantly at the market. And if you had asked my four daughters where vegetables came from, they would have likely said the grocery store. Since I work in food for a living, I know my kids aren't alone in their ignorance, and I can't blame today's youth for not thinking beyond the local market. Our country has fewer farmers than ever before. Never has a population been so far removed from the miracle of food sprouting forth from the earth. We head to the grocery store where the produce aisle is well stocked, and we can buy whatever ingredient our downloaded recipe requests of us. We even get peaches in January, and we are led to believe that food growing from the earth is no big deal—and may not even involve God's hand at all.

God gave us our minds to use and to think, and of course we should use technology, discovery, and scientific knowledge to advance society, including agriculture. The result is an efficiency that means fewer of us need to be farmers. But I worry that this evolution means we have too little knowledge of where our food comes from. Are we so far from the miracle that is food that we don't even recognize it for the miracle it is?

We may be missing out on a giant part of God's best for us when it comes to food. And that ignorance has other consequences. When we don't know anything about how God's earth is gardened, we can't be confident it is being tended in a way that honors God. As consumers, we can easily live in blind trust that tomato workers are paid fairly, that our earth is being treated with respect, and that we are somehow entitled to inexpensive, blemish-free produce at any moment we care to swing by the market, 24-7. In the food media business, we even tell consumers what imperfect produce to reject: Look for a smooth skin on the tomato! Don't pick a cabbage that doesn't feel heavy! Look for a nice cream spot on that watermelon!

But what if instead we pick the tomato that isn't gorgeous, the one we know will be left behind? Even better, as a country, what if we followed France's example and required produce "seconds" sections to encourage shoppers to buy "imperfect" fruits and veggies at a discount? Some stores in the United States do this but not nearly enough. I love that these little miracles that might be rejected by many find a home on the table instead of in a trash bin.

So, if you've never done so, I hope you'll try to grow something to eat—at least once. I know we can't magically connect everyone in a healthy way to our food system, but we can all try to get a little closer to the miracle. Even an indoor herb garden can serve as a daily reminder of our dependence on God, of the gift of patience that gardening fosters, and of our role in the food life cycle. We are the planters and tenders of the garden, but none of our seeds would bear fruit without God.

RSVP to the Invitation into Dependence

- Plant a small herb or vegetable garden from seeds. Notice how they sprout in their own timing, each seed sprouting at a different rate. If you have kids, have them guess which herb will grow from which seed—it's nearly impossible! Watch the daily progress and consider all the invisible work that God is doing beneath the surface. Seeds look nothing like the resulting plant, and this is one of the great reminders of the transformational power of Christ. Think about what seed in your life today needs complete transformation. Pray for God to work in your life as he desires.

- Read the parable of the sower in Luke 8:4–15, in which Jesus used the seed as a metaphor for the Word of God. How and where the Word is planted change its impact. Think about why Jesus would use a gardening analogy to explain God's wisdom. What kind of soil are we offering for his words to take root? Notice the last line of the parable's explanation: we need to persevere to produce a crop. Where is God calling you to have more perseverance?

- Gardens are a place of care, rest, and acceptance of God's provision. The lessons learned in growing food also apply to life. We are the planters and waterers not only of gardens but also of projects, dreams, and ideas. Think of a project or dream you are working on now, and pray for God to give you the willingness to do the necessary work—to plant and to water, to be patient, to acknowledge your dependence on him, and to trust the wisdom of his results.

Chapter 15

Sharing God's Gifts

An Invitation into Hospitality

Biblical hospitality is service,
not performance.

What comes to mind when you think about hospitality? Maybe you start thinking about hosting dinner parties, inviting friends into your home, or searching the internet to download "company worthy" recipes that you'll spend all day making. Maybe even the thought of hosting stresses you out. Perhaps hospitality sounds like something you aren't particularly gifted at, so you leave the hosting work to someone else at church because, hey, each according to her gifts, right? But biblical hospitality is not about impressing, and it's not reserved for the gifted few.

Biblical hospitality is, literally, "love of strangers," and we are all called to practice it. Hospitality is about service to others, not about performance. It is not about impressing our guests with Pinterest-worthy meals. Hospitality is not meant to show off our skills as a cook;

it is about sharing the gift of God's ingredients with others. Hosting gives people space to be themselves and to connect in an authentic, deep way. Can our humble homes and meals really do that even if we aren't particularly gifted cooks, let alone someone on Food Network? Yes. And hospitality is worth the effort.

There is something magical about welcoming people into our homes. Sharing our private living space with others invites intimacy with them and requires our vulnerability. Hosting means we keep our (figurative, but sometimes literal) dirty laundry out for others to see. Guests are privy to our imperfect lives. They see beyond the carefully selected version of imperfection that we post on Instagram. Our guests see the real, live thing, and that's a little scary. In my house, for instance, guests might see the coffee stain on the easy chair that I try to hide with a beige throw or the hole in the huge painting hanging in the dining room that I patched with masking tape and a blue Sharpie. This sharing of ourselves puts others at ease because whenever we see the imperfections of others, we all exhale a bit, knowing we aren't alone in our messes. Sharing our homes reveals our humanness without our saying a word. Being together in a home automatically invites authenticity and gives us all space to connect in deeper ways than if we only met up for coffee at Starbucks, where everything down to the coffeehouse-vibe music playlist is managed for the corporate image. Hospitality isn't about showing off polished perfection; it's about serving strangers to make them feel valued and treasured. No backdrop coaxes out our truest selves better than the imperfect, rich tableau of our homes with its scuffed furniture and coffee mug collection that reveals more about us than we realize.

The Joy of Giving

I learned about hospitality at an early age. When I was five, I discovered the joy of cooking for others and welcoming them into our home. It was just before Christmas. My mom was raising my sister and me on her tight budget, but she was determined to have friends over to celebrate the season. We gathered simple, generic-brand ingredients: margarine, sugar, flour, eggs, baking powder, vanilla. While Mom creamed the margarine, I added the sugar. Measuring, working in sync, Stacy, Mom, and I created a simple sugar-cookie dough. We spooned it onto baking sheets, and in minutes she pulled them from the oven: melt-in-your-mouth cookies, crisp on the bottom but still chewy and just slightly crumbly. They were misshapen and simple, but they were special. Together we'd created a gift we were excited for our friends to share.

Later that day we welcomed our girlfriends—Mom's and ours—into our tiny, unimpressive home. We ate those awkward sugar cookies and sipped hot chocolate made from powdered mix and hot water. We gathered around our dilapidated thrift-store piano, played hesitantly by my sister, and sang carols. We threaded popcorn to make Christmas tree garland. This was not a fete worthy of the society pages or even a paper invitation. But it didn't matter. The joy we shared in being together, celebrating the season with friends and food, made me fall in love with cooking. I saw the ability of food to connect people.

That first holiday gathering brought us such joy that it evolved into an annual event we came to call our Mother-Daughter Holiday Tea. It was an early anthem to girl power before such a thing was ever a hashtag. Some years we would go all out, cooking for weeks ahead of time and stocking our freezer with goodies. Other years, finances or busyness meant we served a threadbare menu of cookies and carrots and celery sticks—which, Mom eventually learned, was called a "crudité," and that fancy word validated her simple buffet. I remember these small details of our early parties, yet none of them really mattered. I learned quickly from Mom that the people were always more important than the food.

Our mother-daughter tea became a tradition treasured not only by us but also by our dearest friends, some of whom only knew one another as regular Christmastime guests over the years. The tea parties marked the passage of my childhood, like pencil marks in the garage denoting the heights of the kids who lived there.

By the time I was in college, Mom was a full-fledged physician. Our tea parties had become quite fancy: sumptuous buffets of gorgeous meat roasts, delicate pastries, and fine champagne-laced mimosas poured into Mom's opaque black crystal goblets we'd bought at the Mikasa outlet. I'd come to love tradition and entertaining, and I learned to count on connecting with my female friends at our mother-daughter teas.

When Mom died my junior year of college, the holiday teas stopped without notice. That first Christmas that I was alone without Mom was even lonelier because I had also lost my yearly touch point with all the significant women in my life. Fortunately, the women who mattered most to me in my mom's absence were local: my mom's best friend, Jerri, and her daughter, Katie, who was exactly my age and had known me since we were six. Jerri invited me to move into their home after I sold Mom's house to pay for her many expenses (suicide exclusions made most of her insurance useless). Jerri encouraged me to start a holiday tea again when I felt ready. I tucked the idea into my heart for nearly two decades.

I knew it was time to revive the mother-daughter tea when I had daughters of my own. In 2006, I baked cookies for my sixteenth mother-daughter tea—the first with my daughters Valentine and Charlotte—and invited local mom friends, who brought their daughters. The very next year, we added the girls' twin sisters, Margaux and Océane, to the guest list. All our girls have come to look forward to the annual party, claiming it's their favorite day of the year. Every September we brainstorm the guest list, which grows each year, since we have a once-invited-always-invited approach to welcoming our favorite girls and women into our house.

In the early days of the d'Arabian tea, I was on a tight budget. I shopped thrift stores to buy old, used porcelain cups—not the dainty vintage kind used in Victorian times to sip Earl Grey tea, but the ugly coffee cups of the 1970s with faded plaid patterns that I snagged for fifty cents apiece. Our collection has grown over the years, and we've added pricier sweet teacups with painted flowers and fancy designs. But I keep the ugly ducklings from the early days to render their mishmash mark on our party.

The food we serve, even the simplest dishes, brings everyone together, and some dishes are perennial favorites. The chocolate fountain has become a much-anticipated feature, both by all our party guests and, in anticipation of the postparty tradition, by all our family members: we allow the girls to stick their tongues directly into the warm flowy chocolate before it gets thrown out. My potato-bacon torte with its flaky butter crust gets rave reviews, and repeat guests ask for it when they come in the door. We don't serve anything fussy. Just finger food—and this is the secret to a party rich in hugs! No one is settled into a sit-down meal, and even our hands aren't busy with a knife-and-fork setup. When arms are freed up, women hug more.

Shedding "Martha" Tendencies

The first tea I hosted after winning *The Next Food Network Star* was in Seattle, where we had moved for Philippe's job, and that tea was a lesson in the true meaning of hospitality. The day before the tea, a Pacific Northwest wind and rainstorm caused our pipes to burst. I was new to the city, the guests were recent friends, and, inside my heart, I wanted to impress them. I wanted them to think I was worthy of being the Food Network host that I now was. With our broken pipes, however, the likelihood of that happening declined by the moment.

The emergency plumber we called did his best to fix the problem, but there was simply no way I could do any cooking in time. None. In an attempt to avert a total tea-party catastrophe, I sent my husband to the local grocery store just before it closed at midnight. He raced around the store grabbing anything that seemed tea-party-like. He came home with a pretty sad assortment of rejected birthday cakes, day-old grocery-store cookies, and even some Chips Ahoy!, which he thought looked more homemade than Oreos. The next morning, I tried to keep my spirits up as I arranged industrial-produced chocolate chip cookies on my prettiest platter and gingerly wiped the words *Happy Birthday* off a refrigerated cake. I brewed coffee and set out our motley collection of cups. I then greeted guests with a smile as they walked in the door, re-minding myself that Julia Child believed in never apologizing for the food. The disappointment was the cook's to bear alone. And I was defi-nitely bearing disappointment. And embarrassment.

To add to the dreary mood, the rain was unrelenting. Our house was at the top of a tiny dirt road that wound at least a quarter mile up a steep hill. We had a wonderful view of the lake, but only four or five cars fit in the driveway. Our guests—wearing high-tea dresses and heels—would have to park down below and walk uphill ten minutes in the pelting rain. Except that Philippe, who usually sneaks away during the tea to watch a movie or play a game of tennis with a buddy, offered to act as valet. He shuttled every single guest up the hill and then parked their cars for them. Yes, he went up and down the hill for all three hours of the party. No sooner had the stragglers finished arriving at the party than the early departures began.

This party was set up to be a complete disaster. But guess what? None of this mattered to anyone. What could have been a disastrous party ended up a being a total joy. If anyone cared that we dared to serve doughnuts from a supermarket box (cringe!), I couldn't tell. At that very tea, people connected and laughed and talked, and I made friends whom I still have today. That day I shed some of my "Martha" tendencies—and by Martha I'm referring to the biblical story of sisters Martha and Mary who hosted Jesus in their home, not Martha Stewart, although I shed those expectations too. The Martha in the Bible was overly concerned about the details of entertaining her guests, while Mary focused on Jesus. When Martha complained about her sister not helping but rather sitting and listening to Jesus talk, he told Martha that Mary was the one whose heart was actually in the right place. On that rainy, muddy, broken-pipes day, God saved me from becoming Martha in my hosting, and he redeemed the disaster by opening my eyes to being in the presence of precious friends.

Have you ever had a last-minute disaster you thought would ruin a party or gathering? I'll bet it didn't. And even if it did, I'll bet you realized gifts from that event that couldn't have possibly happened without that hiccup. The good news is that the point of the party is never for the host to look good. The objective is and has always been to serve those who come into our homes. When I look back, I realize that some of my hosting mishaps helped reorient me toward this sacred purpose.

The Most Important Thing We Offer

The first year the girls were finally old enough to help set up the food on the tables, I was thrilled. But about a half hour before the start of the party, all four of them had abandoned their stations. I was annoyed as I looked for them—we had so much left to do! I found them standing outside in the front yard, ready to greet any guests who arrived early. I smiled and instantly made the rule for myself in entertaining that if I'm too busy in the kitchen to greet my guests at the door, I need to simplify my menu. Does that ever happen to you? You can't leave the kitchen to open the door to let your guests in? If so, I offer this thought: the most important thing we give our guests is our attention and love. The food is a conduit, certainly, but it's secondary. People matter more than the platters on the buffet table.

When the girls were in preschool, kindergarten, and first grade, respectively, we moved to Coronado, California, a small town known for its beaches and two naval bases. But to our daughters, who had attended only a small, private French-American school in Seattle, attending public school for the first time in a new town felt daunting. The girls knew no one in their classes, and we all felt a little untethered. A small town can seem extra overwhelming because being on the outside of an everyone-knows-everyone village can feel lonelier than being part of the shared anonymity of a big city.

We decided to invite each girl's classmates and their families over for hot chocolate and coffee, hosting a separate event for each girl's class. Because of our work schedules, we knew we couldn't have a complicated event, or it would never happen. And let me tell you something: it's hard not to go too crazy whipping up television-worthy dishes when you are new to town and everyone knows you as the Food Network lady. What would they think if I served them food from a bakery and not from my own oven? I fought every urge I had to worry about what my new neighbors would think of me serving store-bought goodies instead of Martha Stewart-ing my way through the situation. Philippe and I kept it truly simple: we made name tags, brewed pots of coffee, heated water for the cocoa, and bought bagels and cut fruit at Costco. The "classroom coffees"—as we called them—were so basic that I was almost embarrassed.

But something unexpected happened. Playing together and nibbling precut fruit in our living room and the backyard created a community that carried over into the classroom. Our daughters all felt they were part of something after hosting their classmates in our homes—so much so that we made our classroom coffees an annual tradition. Even though the girls were no longer the new kids at school, their sense of belonging was always stronger after the classroom event—not only because we opened our home and offered food but also because we offered the families some love by simply serving them. Even arranging food on a platter and then cleaning up the dirty dishes afterward are service.

Just as I learned from my mother, my daughters have learned from me the beauty of hospitality and community. Sharing food connects us and reminds us how similar we really are despite our human-created societal constructs. As a result, our hearts are more open, and there is space for the Holy Spirit to do his work. Think back to some of your favorite moments with friends, those moments of deep connection that tell you this relationship is real and it matters. I'll bet food was involved in many of those moments!

Sharing food and welcoming people into our homes invite relation-ship. We don't have to host fancy teas or large gatherings. We can have just one or two people sharing a simple meal and an authentic connec-tion. In fact, we bought a comfy couch set for our porch specifically to encourage us to invite friends to our home for coffee instead of meeting out. Whenever practical, we invite our daughters' after-school playdates to stay for dinner because even ten-year-olds open up more at the table. Sunday afternoons are a perfect slot for our family to host a small gath-ering. Sometimes it's an invite to come for lemonade and cookies, and then if I get around to making anything above that, it's a bonus. Some-times we just host another family for a big slow-cooker pot of black bean soup. Hospitality is serving others, not impressing them.

We can all host even if cooking isn't our natural gift. In fact, we are told specifically to host: "Offer hospitality to one another without grumbling" (1 Peter 4:9). We can follow Jesus's example. He welcomed all—foreigners, strangers, people who were different from him—into his fold. We can take comfort in knowing that at any given moment, we are actually being hosted ourselves by God! Whatever we do here on earth, we are doing at the invitation of God as his guests. Whether we go to the movies, take our kids to soccer, or host an annual mother-daughter tea, all we do happens on God's turf anyway. So take comfort in knowing the pressure is off. Just welcome and serve. The gift of hos-pitality allows authentic selves to come out of hiding, and that is the result of loving, not dazzling.

RSVP to the Invitation into Hospitality

- We see a good example of biblical hospitality in Genesis 18:1–15. It's the story of Abraham and Sarah welcoming in strangers, who—unbeknownst to them—turn out to be angels and God himself. Take note of some characteristics of their hospitality. How does this example change how you want to welcome people?

- Hospitality isn't just inviting our friends over; it's loving strangers well too. Consider how you might be able to extend hospitality to people who aren't yet friends and to people who are different from you. Perhaps welcome the neighbors you've been meaning to meet or a family from church you don't know yet, or even just sit outside with a pot of coffee and chat with a stranger walking by.

- Remove from your hospitality vocabulary any language that separates you from others. Think how you describe hosting even to yourself. Do you look for dishes that "impress" or "dazzle" or "make your friends think you spent a lot of time when you didn't"? Language like this tells us that we are performing, not serving, and that our goal is for our guests to put us on a pedestal and think great things of us. So, instead of separating ourselves from guests by making them feel like *I could never do this*, make unity and acceptance the goal of all your hospitality. Think of your hospitality as creating a space for God to join in. Start noticing if your language reflects that goal.

Chapter 16

Reflecting Our Values by How We Eat

An Invitation into the Sacred

Our meal rituals reflect our
lives and are opportunities for
growing into our true selves.

The long view of our lives is that we are preparing for the eternal life we will live with our Maker in heaven. The gifts of this earth can serve as a glimpse into life lived in harmony with God, and so those gifts matter. In fact, the very actions surrounding our meals can be theological practices that draw us closer to God. For instance, when we say grace before a meal, we get to express our gratitude and acknowledge our dependence on God to feed us. These practices shape us more than we think as they spill over into our daily lives. Dinner is more than a loading zone for nutrition; it's a glimpse into our lives as a whole. Your childhood dinner memories probably take you straight back to who you were fundamentally as a family, away from the table. Meals aren't just about food—the spaces in which we share them matter. Perhaps the most sacred space in the house is the dining room table.

When I was growing up, we ate every single meal at our old wooden kitchen table. (We didn't have a dining room.) We kept that same pressboard wooden table until I was a teenager. We repainted it ourselves every few years without ever sanding it down, thickening the surface coating as the years went by. When I see pictures of my childhood in an old photo album, I can always identify the era by the color of that table: first it was cream, then white, then sunshine yellow, and finally a bright, almost neon, green, which looked messy and gloppy even in those faded photos.

I can't think about that table without clearly recalling the plates and dishes we used for serving the food. Even they shaped my childhood. Mom's Friday fish belonged in the thirteen-by-nine-inch Pyrex pan, alongside her lemon-buttered potatoes cooked in CorningWare and scooped onto our unbreakable white Corelle plates. What I understood from my childhood was that in an uncertain world, our table was a place of remarkable consistency. As a kid I never got to try exotic food like sushi, but I never had to wonder if tacos would show up on a Monday night. Mom always made it happen, even in tough times.

The table is so much more than a piece of furniture. It's a place where we work out our identity, sitting with the same people day after day, year after year. The table is a witness to the worthy work of meals: setting the table, saying grace, cleaning the dishes. And the table is witness to families growing, people arriving and leaving, and life being lived.

The Place Where We Are Ourselves

Every summer, I spent a month visiting my paternal grandparents in Southern California. Even there, in their relatively palatial home, their plain brown Ethan Allen shaker kitchen table was my favorite spot. No matter what time I would wake up, I knew both my grandparents would be parked at the kitchen table, sipping weak coffee and watching—on the lowest volume—Regis and Kathie Lee or some other morning program. Their toaster sat on that table—which struck me as not only convenient but highbrow—alongside an array of breads and jams from Knott's Berry Farm. Orange juice was already poured into tiny juice cups, and oatmeal sat warm on the stove, just in case having some struck my fancy. Setting out food that wasn't sure to be eaten was the kind of luxury reserved for a different economic class altogether, which is probably why I felt not the least bit conflicted about letting my friends at home know that my grandparents were rich. (They were not.)

What I loved most about Grandma's breakfast table was the lingering. Grandma told me stories about her younger days and falling in love with Grandpa at the age of six. Grandpa would steal my orange juice, and I'd pretend I didn't know it was him. We all played our roles to their fullest—the cute blonde granddaughters in matching dresses, tights, and pigtails, and the doting grandparents who casually set out candy dishes filled with M&M's around the house for an anytime treat and who gave us hot-fudge sundaes every night after dinner.

Dinners at Grandma's, though, happened in the dining room at a table covered with both a dark tablecloth and a lace coverlet and always set with heavy china. We'd eat hearty German dishes and stews, and we drank Pepsi in thick green-footed glasses. I loved it second to the kitchen table. Because it was fancier, the dining room table often meant guests, which was festive, but at breakfast we didn't have to share Grandma and Grandpa with anyone.

When I was in high school, I was in a play called *The Dining Room* by A. R. Gurney. It's a collection of scenes that play out over generations in one dining room. The piece is moving because it recalls both the nostalgic passage of time and the room that bore witness to it all: joy, sorrow, connection, and loss. The play resonated deeply with me because the table was the first place I remember understanding who I was and how I fit into the family, and it was the place where my family identity was solidified over and over. Our old wooden kitchen table anchored me.

When I turned thirty, I gave myself the gift of a custom-made dining set—a shabby-chic brush-painted antique reproduction—that fit my Santa Monica apartment perfectly. I had just gotten a raise at Disney, and that table signified my move to adulthood. I invited my seven best girl-friends over to celebrate with a pink dinner party: I served salmon with beets and horseradish and, for dessert, a raspberry tart, all of which looked gorgeous against the table's off-white surface. The table helped me define myself yet again: a thirty-year-old finance executive with an enviable rent-controlled apartment and friends who were truly family.

A year later, when I moved to Paris with my job with Disney, I insisted on taking my dining table with me, and it took up like 90 percent of the tiny crate I'd been allocated for my overseas move. The crate finally arrived in France about a month after I did. The movers couldn't get the table through the incredibly skinny doorways of the old building where I lived, so they came up with their own solution and sawed off a fourth of the table to make it slim enough to fit. They just lopped off a big chunk of table, never thinking to run this idea by me, and left both pieces for me in the living room. I was incredulous and devastated and outraged, but I didn't have the French language skills to take up the fight, so I didn't.

I tried living with it, but I couldn't look at the table without tearing up, so I finally gave it away to a sweet Australian expat named Callie, a new friend who didn't have a table at all. She and I stayed fast friends for all four years I lived in France. Somehow, seeing my ruined table in her apartment didn't upset me as much, and I think having it helped her figure out who she was as a stranger in a new country. Some things are meant to be passed along, even if it's a table with a sawed-off edge.

When Philippe and I married, we invested in a huge Mexican wood table that took up half our apartment but could seat up to ten people. We were part of the young professional pulse of Paris who regularly had dinners together that started at ten o'clock, even on work nights. Philippe cooked as often as I did—maybe even more—a habit we picked up when I was working crazy-long hours at Disney with an hour-and-a-half commute each way. He would make gorgeous *magrets de canard en croûte,* a duck breast wrapped in a salty dough and baked just until the meat was tender and pink, the crust cut away and discarded. Or I would go deep into my West Coast roots and grill up a fajitas feast complete with homemade roasted salsa and guacamole. I learned quickly to tame down the spice. The French love fine food, but hot chilies aren't as universally adored in Paris as they are in Los Angeles.

When we had kids, I was ready for the slower pace and earlier start times of family dinners. Our family table has always been the center of our family life, and I wouldn't have it any other way. From the time the older kids could walk and help me feed their baby sisters, our table and the food we served there have played a central role in our language of love.

The benefits of living around a table affect all areas of our lives. Whoever has the task of setting the table gets the gift of slowing down and learning the joy of serving others. When we say grace, we pause to acknowledge our dependence on God and the work behind the food, and we get to practice gratitude as we thank him. Our family policy of having one conversation at a time around the table gives us all valuable training in listening to others. When one of our daughters has had a bad day, the dinner table at mealtime is a soft place for her to lay her heart, and the others get to practice coming alongside their sister in compassion. The girls even take turns making school lunches on our table, and they get to practice hospitality and thoughtfulness. The table has become an emblem of our family identity. The day my daughter wanted to tell us she had her first boyfriend, she excitedly called everyone to the table, the only place fitting to share every single detail of such big news. And three months later when that relationship ended, we helped her process it at the table.

Who we are at the table says a lot about who we are away from the table. If we are mindful and considerate around the table simply because of habit, liturgy, or even house rules, those muscles will be practiced and strong, ready to help us be mindful and considerate in real life. Holding the table as a special space pays dividends by bringing us closer to being the grateful, kind, generous people we'd all like to be.

The Spiritual Essence of Purposeful Eating

Families and food and modern life don't always allow for sweet little examples of God-honoring eating at its best. We live in a world of fast food, quick answers, self-reliance, and divisiveness. The world of social media and constant "connectivity" can fool us into thinking we are connected even when we aren't. We can trick ourselves into thinking we are part of a community when we are simply together in being alone. The beauty of eating at a table is that we connect, we share, we define and strengthen our values, and we practice spirituality at a deeper level.

Stopping long enough to sit around a table is quickly becoming an antiquated notion, though, especially once kids become busy teenagers with lives and friends of their own. Our parents' generation stopped to share a Coke or milkshake at the local dime store where they sat at the counter and talked to one another. Teens now grab coffee drinks (essentially milkshakes, twice the size)—no sharing—and they keep on walking in this sip-and-step culture that fosters mindless consumption. My girls recently discovered the joy of registering Starbucks gift cards online. Now they can preorder their drinks, relieving them of those pesky five or ten minutes chatting together in line. They just grab their sugary drinks and run off, stopping long enough to catch a cute selfie to post or text their friends. And let's be honest: this pace is not just the kids'. I get caught up in the grab-and-go culture too.

But time at the table is worth fighting for! The table is the touch point for our day. Sometimes it's the only chance we'll have to connect with our loved ones. It's a space to pause for a moment, reflect, recharge, and reinforce our sense of self. The table is a cornerstone of so many spiritual practices, including gratitude, dependence, self-control, and patience. Adding more table time to our lives will only benefit us.

Hope for Reflecting Our Spiritual Values

How we eat says a lot about what we value, and sitting down to enjoy food around a shared table is holy. Those tables are a microcosm of our very lives. The energy and work it takes to make our tables and meals affirming and life giving is worthy work—as God intended. We don't have to be perfect, and the meals don't have to be either. God doesn't call us to perfection. He doesn't even call us to be great. He just calls us to be obedient. And there is so much grace for the imperfection of our obedience.

So, are you craving a meal that only Domino's can deliver? I've been there, sister. Go ahead: order it and then sit down with your family around the table, because part of the magic of the meal is in being at the table together. Maybe next time you're at Starbucks with friends, sit with your drink to be with people—to truly be with them, not your phone—before you race out the door.

More than anything, food has been for me an invitation into tasting God's boundless, beautiful grace. That, my dear friend, is worth savoring.

RSVP to the Invitation into the Sacred

- Next time you have dinner, notice the details that are actually small spiritual practices: from setting the table to saying grace to cleaning up the dishes. What does each one of these actions do to draw us closer to God?
- In Psalm 23:5, a discouraged David finds comfort and strength in God: "You prepare a table before me in the presence of my enemies. You anoint my head with oil; my cup overflows." The table that God sets for us *is* his presence, strength, and comfort. Sit at the table or counter where you eat the most often. Reflect on the meals and conversations you've had

there and the ways those times helped shape your identity and values. Think about the role that table has played in so many important moments in your life. In what ways has God used your simple, humble table to make himself known to you and your family?

- Life is busy, and meals sometimes happen on the run. Try adding one more shared meal a week to your routine. Maybe that means getting up a few minutes early to have a family breakfast before school. Or if you live alone, maybe you invite some neighbors to share a meal at the table once a week. Sit around the table and simply share a meal. Do you notice that sharing a meal is actually sharing life?

Final Thoughts

f I ever wondered why God brought food into my life in such a big
way, boldly letting this non-chef-cook win a major food competition
and host her own show on Food Network, the exercise in writing this
book solved any lingering mystery. For me, food has been the catalyst
for deep connection with God. He is no longer a theoretical Big-Brother-
like being whom I imagine hovering over us all. Neither is he an on-the-
ground but elusive presence, like the hologram ghosts at Disneyland's
Haunted Mansion. God is here, working in this world, right this minute,
and he is using—among other things—food for his glory.

Competing on *The Next Food Network Star* helped me find my
identity as a creator when I was forced to trust the ingredients and focus
on God in the midst of all the noise. I learned about hospitality being
service, not performance, from my mom's simple mother-daughter teas.
Katy Rudder's Fritos and my elementary school secretary gave me dignity and showed me how sharing food and space at the table can restore
oneness and equality. Libby's olive-and-egg dip in Mom's recipe box
connected me with my past, and a childhood eating on a limited budget turned me into a good steward. Who would guess that making
brownies could be redemptive and help me heal after losing Mom to
suicide, or that a night of overindulging in red wine could introduce me

to God's abundant grace? Marrying a French man introduced me to patience in my meals and gave me space to pause. Feeding my babies gave me a glimpse of the nurturing love God has for his own children and helped me trust his love more. Becoming a "celebrity chef" ironically gave me humility, by reminding me of my dependence on God.

I'm getting better at delighting in the food God has created, and I finally can accept and even love who I am today, striving to glorify God with my body, not striving to gain a body that could be on a magazine cover. I'm redefining the work of the kitchen as worship, and most days I am filled with more joy than dread when 5:00 p.m. rolls around. More telling, I'm willing to do the dishes with a happy heart, and, frankly, that's the part of cooking I've always struggled with. I'm celebrating my role as a planter and waterer, leaning into dependence on God for food and for everything else. And I'm honoring the sacred space of our family table, placing a higher priority on family dinners and the simple liturgy of eating around a table. These times are now more precious than ever, given the short number of years I'll have with all four girls at home before they move out to live their own lives.

Compassion, comfort, creation, authenticity, grace, patience, connection, nurturing, stewardship, humility, work, delight, acceptance, dependence, hospitality, and the sacred—these are gifts from God and characteristics of theological eating. But they are also something bigger and more important. They are invitations that God issues through food—invitations to lean more fully into him and to experience grace that is so delicious we can literally taste it, our deepest spiritual hunger satisfied.

How we respond is up to us.

Acknowledgments

Thanking everyone who helped birth a book is always an emotional experience. I have extra gratitude in my heart to the team that made this one happen.

First, I want to thank my agent, Margaret Riley King, who believed in this project even when I couldn't put it into words. I'm so grateful that she believed in me even in moments when I didn't.

To the entire team at WaterBrook: Campbell Wharton, Laura Barker, Susan Tjaden, Kimberly Von Fange, Beverly Rykerd, Lisa Beech, Johanna Inwood, and Kelly Howard, thank you for making this book happen and for shepherding me through the process of writing without a recipe. Special thanks to my editor, Susan, who always knew just the tweak to suggest to solve my writing woes. Thank you for bringing Ginger Kolbaba into my life. Ginger, I am forever grateful for your input and keen editing eye. Ami McConnell, I'm blessed by your vision, editing, and your friendship. Amy Paulson, you are one of my favorite friends. Thank you for photographing me.

A big thank-you to Norman Wirzba, whose writing has both educated and inspired me and whose friendship has surprised and delighted me. Thank you to Rachel Marie Stone, Tim Chester, and Kendall Vanderslice for writing words that changed me.

I'm lucky to have cheerleaders who inspired me to continue on the path. Thank you, Angela Robles, Lisa Johnson, Rachel Hollis, Aarti Sequeira, Elizabeth Wampler, Drew and Heather Goodmanson, Jamey and Nicole Cohen, and Donna and Allen Frances. Thank you, my dear friend Mindy Williams, for inspiring the title that helped everything fall into place.

Finally, and most importantly, I'm grateful to my family. Philippe, Océane, Margaux, Charlotte, and Valentine: you are in my heart, in my soul, and in every breath I took while writing this book.